UK Foreign and Asylum Policy

Human Rights Audit

2001

Amnesty International UK

NOTE:

Amnesty International uses the standard international definitions of human rights as set out in the Universal Declaration of Human Rights and subsequently in the laws and standards detailed in international treaties such as the International Covenant on Civil and Political Rights, the International Covenant on Economic, Social and Cultural Rights, and in the Geneva Conventions and other instruments of humanitarian law. These international standards make it clear what individuals' human rights are and the role and responsibilities of governments in protecting these.

Human Rights Audit 2001
UK Foreign and Asylum Policy

September 2001
©Amnesty International United Kingdom
99-119 Rosebery Avenue
London EC1R 4RE

Printed by Centurion Press Ltd

ISBN 1-873328-47-8
AIUK Product Code PB252

Photographs
Cover: *Rwanda – rebel soldier* © Crispin Hughes/ Panos Pictures
Page 9 *Kosovo – British troops* © Andrew Testa/ Panos Pictures
Page 17 *Chechnya – Grozny under Russian occupation* © Leo Erken/ Panos Pictures
Page 26 *Iraq – Kurdish mother and child, Ranya hospital* © Peter Chappell/ Panos Pictures
Page 38 *Bosnia-Herzegovina – search for the remains of victims of ethnic cleansing* © Paul Lowe/ Magnum (*AI 2001 Media Award winner*)
Page 42 *United Kingdom – National Front demonstration, Margate* © David Hoffman
Page 48 *Italy – destruction of Romani dwelling, Casilina 700 camp, Rome* © Stefano Montesi
Page 57 *Indonesia – troops in Jakarta prepare to move into Aceh* © Dermot Tatlow/ Panos Pictures
Page 60 *Mozambique – Red Cross landmine awareness theatre* © Heldur Netocny/ Panos Pictures
Page 67 *Palestinian Authority – Fatah demonstration* © Chris Stowers/ Panos Pictures
Page 81 *United Kingdom – Prayer booklet, a refugee's reminder of family* © Jenny Matthews

Contents

1 Overview

International diplomacy 5
International justice 6
Asylum policy 6
Business and human rights 7

2 International diplomacy

The commitment to human rights 10
Human rights culture in Whitehall 10
Annual reports 12
Critical engagement 12
Case studies 14
Military responses 18
Human rights themes 20
The UK and multilateral organisations 22
Recommendations 29

3 International justice

The Pinochet case 30
The international criminal tribunals 31
The International Criminal Court 33
Challenges for Labour's second term 36
Recommendations 37

4 Asylum policy

The early years: the 1998 white paper and the 1999 bill 39
Asylum determination procedures 40
Access to legal advice 41
Appeals on human rights grounds 43
Racial discrimination 44
Detention of asylum seekers 44
Libyan asylum applicants 46
European and international developments 46
Prospects for the second term 49
Recommendations 51

5 Business and human rights 52

Controlling the arms trade 52
Corporate policies and practice 64
Recommendations 65

Appendix

Human rights in the United Kingdom:
Briefing to the UN Human Rights Committee, July 2001 68
Endnotes 82
The work of Amnesty International 84

1 Overview

1.1 'The Labour Government will put human rights at the heart of our foreign policy,' the foreign secretary declared on 12 May 1997, soon after the government was elected. Amnesty International welcomed the government's pledge. We believed that the commitment was important as a matter of principle and that it was in the UK's strategic interest. The violation of human rights is a catalyst for armed conflicts and refugee flows that affect the UK, as has been demonstrated during the past decade by events in the Balkans, the Middle East, Asia and elsewhere.

1.2 This report is the fourth in an annual series examining the extent to which the government did indeed respect and promote human rights in its foreign policy. The report looks at Labour's first term in office, from May 1997 to June 2001, and some key events since the general election of 2001.

1.3 The report also examines the government's policy towards asylum seekers in the light of international human rights standards. Other areas of domestic policy are outside the ambit of this report but have been documented elsewhere. An overview of Amnesty International's concerns about human rights within the UK is provided in an Appendix.

International diplomacy

1.4 The government made significant positive contributions in some areas, including:
• providing assistance in response to human rights crises, for example in East Timor, Kosovo and Sierra Leone;
• campaigning for the abolition of the death penalty internationally;
• establishing a Human Rights Project Fund that has assisted hundreds of projects around the world, on issues including torture, caste violence and impunity;
• helping to develop European Union guidelines on discouraging torture in non-EU countries.

1.5 Amnesty International has reservations and concerns about the policies pursued in some other areas. For example, the government has sought 'critical engagement' with countries that systematically violate internationally recognised human rights. It has tried to encourage reform through dialogue and advice while maintaining diplomatic, commercial and cultural relations. Critical engagement may be a constructive approach where the other country acknowledges that its human rights record is deficient and is committed to reform. However, there is a danger that critical engagement becomes a mask for 'business as usual', with only lip service being paid to human rights. This danger is exacerbated when the government establishes a formal human rights dialogue, as it has with China. Without a genuine commitment to change, such dialogues will be ineffective. In China, respect for fundamental civil and political rights has deteriorated since the human rights dialogue began, yet the UK has failed significantly to amend its policy in response.

1.6 As was the case with previous governments, the Labour government has muted its statements on the human rights record of the government of Saudi Arabia. This reflects the primacy given to that country's economic and strategic importance to the UK. Again, Amnesty International considers that the government must use fora such as the UN Commission on Human Rights to hold Saudi Arabia publicly accountable.

1.7 Amnesty International was pleased to note that Labour's 2001 election manifesto pledged that in foreign policy the government would continue to encourage universal observance of human rights. In his first major speech as foreign secretary, Jack Straw stated the government's commitment to work for human rights. Amnesty International urges him to underline this commitment by setting out in detail his strategy and priorities.

Key recommendations
■ The foreign secretary should underline his commitment to human rights by setting out his strategy and priorities.

■ The House of Commons foreign affairs committee should continue to conduct an annual inquiry into the government's performance in promoting and protecting human rights.

■ The foreign secretary should publish a detailed statement on 'human rights dialogues', describing among things:
• the criteria for determining that human rights dialogues are appropriate;
• how the objectives for progress and timescales are determined;
• procedures for assessing progress.

International justice

1.8   The government actively supported the international criminal tribunals for the former Yugoslavia and Rwanda. It also played a key role in negotiations for the treaty to establish a permanent International Criminal Court (ICC) and facilitated the passage of legislation by Westminster to enable the UK to ratify the treaty. Ratification is now subject to the passage of complementary legislation by the Scottish parliament.

1.9   Amnesty International has welcomed the legislation, which puts the UK on track to be a founder-member of the ICC. However, there are weaknesses in the UK law. For example, although the treaty specifies that state and diplomatic immunity cannot shield a person from prosecution, the legislation permits the secretary of state, in any particular case, to respect a person's state or diplomatic immunity and order that no proceedings be taken to transfer that individual to the ICC.

1.10   Amnesty International urges the government to ratify the treaty as soon as possible after the Scottish parliament passes its legislation, to continue its efforts to persuade other countries to do so, and to strengthen the UK legislation.

Key recommendations
■ The government should continue to provide financial, diplomatic and practical support for the international criminal tribunals for the former Yugoslavia and Rwanda.

■ The government, bilaterally and through the EU, should continue to encourage other countries to ratify the treaty to establish the ICC.

■ The secretary of state should make an order to bring the ICC Act 2001 into force at the earliest opportunity.

■ The UK government should amend the International Criminal Court Act 2001
• to provide for domestic jurisdiction over all persons present in the UK;
• to ensure that the victims of ICC offences tried in the UK can receive compensation or support if the perpetrators are unable to pay.
The Scottish Executive and MSPs should introduce these amendments into the Scottish bill on the ICC.

Asylum policy

1.11   Amnesty International has been dismayed by various aspects of the UK's treatment of people seeking asylum in the UK. Despite well-documented evidence of grave human rights violations in the countries from which UK-bound asylum seekers predominantly originate, asylum policy was driven by concerns about the number of applicants and whether or not they were 'genuine'.

1.12   Pre-entry controls were strengthened, welfare entitlements were paid as vouchers rather than in cash and applicants were sent to reside in areas ill-equipped to meet their needs, such as specialist legal advice. A new application form was introduced to speed up decision-making but many people failed to complete it within the 10 days permitted and their applications were automatically rejected on the grounds of 'non-compliance'. This reduced the politically sensitive backlog of unprocessed applications, but as many rejected applicants are likely to have appealed, they would have added to the growing backlog at that stage of the determination process.

1.13   The number of people held in detention, often in prisons housing convicted criminals, increased substantially. Legislation was passed in 1999 to provide everyone held in detention with a bail hearing, but the provision is not yet in force and at the time of writing an implementation date has yet to be announced.

1.14   In 2000, legislation to prohibit racial discrimination by public bodies explicitly excluded immigration and asylum decision-making. In July 2001, UK immigration officials were placed in Prague airport to prevent people from boarding flights to the UK if it appeared they might intend to claim asylum. The action was clearly directed against Roma, targets of persistent persecution in the Czech Republic.

1.15   European Union member states began a process of harmonising their refugee and asylum policies. Reports on some of their initial deliberations caused Amnesty International and others to be concerned that to reach agreement, governments may be willing to compromise on standards and weaken protection for asylum seekers.

1.16   Labour's 2001 manifesto committed Britain to continuing to provide a home for people fleeing persecution and also to increase the number of people who are deported when their applications are refused. Events since the election make it impossible to assess how the overall quality of protection for asylum seekers will develop. Amnesty International urges the government to take a fresh look at its asylum policy, and to adopt policies and practices that are consistent with the UK's obligations towards the victims of human rights violations, rather than predicated on the perception of asylum seekers as a 'problem'.

Key recommendations
■ The standard period within which an asylum seeker must complete a Statement of Evidence Form should be extended.

■ Asylum seekers should not be required to live in areas where they cannot have ready access to expert legal advice relating to their claims.

■ The Race Relations Act should be amended to prohibit public officials from discriminating on the grounds of race in the exercise of their functions on matters relating to immigration and asylum.

■ In view of the hardship it involves, detention should be avoided. No asylum seeker should be detained unless it has been established that detention is lawful and complies with intenational standards.

■ Asylum seekers should not be detained in prisons with people convicted of criminal offences.

■ The UK government should take a leading role in advocating that EU member states translate their expressed commitment to international refugee and human rights obligations into specific standards that ensure maximum protection for refugees.

Business and human rights

1.17   Serious deficiencies in legislative and non-legislative controls on the transfer of arms and weapons-manufacturing technology were well known when Labour was elected. Indeed, in opposition Labour had strongly supported the recommendations of the 1996 Scott inquiry into the so-called arms-to-Iraq scandal. However, it did not introduce legislation to strengthen arms export controls until June 2001, after its election to a second term. The legislation provides a framework for control. It is not known how

effective the reforms will be until secondary legislation has been formulated.

1.18   There were a number of welcome non-legislative initiatives. For example, the government banned the export and transhipment of certain equipment used for torture and ill treatment; it introduced new guidelines for the assessment of export licence applications – with respect for human rights in the country of destination as a criterion; it published annual reports on licences granted and took the lead in pressing for the introduction of EU-wide arms controls.

1.19   However, it has adamantly refused to permit Parliament to scrutinise applications for the export of weapons – a system in place in other countries. Amnesty International also considers that the government should strengthen the monitoring of the use of weapons in countries to which they are exported, where there are concerns that they may be used to commit or facilitate human rights violations. Israel is a particular case in point.

1.20   With respect to trade more generally, the government implemented several measures designed to promote awareness and respect for human rights by UK companies. For example, occupational pension funds were required to disclose whether or not social, environmental or ethical considerations are taken into account in the selection and retention of investments. The initiatives are helping to change business culture, but without a strong compliance framework there is insufficient incentive for companies to change their behaviour.

Key recommendations
■ The government should introduce in the next parliamentary session a system of prior parliamentary scrutiny of applications for the export of arms and security equipment.

■ The government should use powers provided under the Export Control and Non-proliferation Bill to impose controls on agents who transport arms and security equipment, even when the UK is not the country of origin, transit or destination. Every shipment should require a licence and a licence for the delivery of arms and security equipment should not be granted where there is a clear risk that the transfer will contribute to violations of human rights and humanitarian law.

■ Licensed production deals should be subject to the same forms of scrutiny and approval that apply to direct exports.

■ The government should revise UK company

law to provide that:
• company directors have a duty to consider the interests of all those affected by their companies' operations, globally, and not only the interests of shareholders;
• directors have a responsibility for the activities of the companies' overseas subsidiaries and partnerships;
• companies are required to report on social, environmental and ethical aspects of their activities in their annual reports.

Sources of information

1.21   Most of the information on which this report is based is taken from:
• the government's public statements and reports;
• information and evidence submitted to parliament;
• the reports of parliamentary committees;
• communications from the government to Amnesty International;
• Amnesty International's observation of UK conduct at inter-governmental meetings and of the operation of UK projects and actions in individual countries;
• monitoring by Amnesty International and other non-governmental organisations of asylum policy in the UK and of human rights in countries throughout the world.

2 International diplomacy

The commitment to human rights

2.1   Soon after his appointment as foreign secretary in May 1997, Robin Cook unveiled a mission statement for the Foreign and Commonwealth Office (FCO). This stated that, among other things, the FCO would 'work through our international forums and bilateral relationships to spread the values of human rights, civil liberties and democracy which we demand for ourselves'.[1]

2.2   Introducing the statement, Mr Cook said that 'our foreign policy must have an ethical dimension and must support the demands of other peoples for the democratic rights on which we insist for ourselves. The Labour government will put human rights at the heart of our foreign policy'.

2.3   The use of the term 'ethical dimension' was immediately controversial. Journalists anticipated inconsistencies and contradictions, with foreign policy becoming lost in a moral maze. Some observers asked whether there was any room for ethics in foreign affairs. Others measured individual decisions against the 'ethical foreign policy', corrupting the phrase that was actually used.

2.4   In consequence, 'ethical' dropped out of the foreign secretary's lexicon. Human rights nevertheless remained a prominent theme until the 2001 general election. In his last major speech on the subject, in March 2001, Robin Cook emphasised two key messages that recurred throughout his term of office:
• It is in the national interest to work for human rights – countries that respect the rights of their own citizens are more likely to be good trading partners and less likely to threaten international stability and UK security.
• The UK's inability to make a difference everywhere should not be used as an excuse for not trying to make a difference where it can do so.[2]

2.5   Following the June 2001 election, the Queen's Speech included a commitment to 'work to encourage universal observance of human rights, including throughout the Commonwealth'. In his first major speech as foreign secretary, on 22 June, Jack Straw said that the government would 'continue to uphold the values which underpin our own security and prosperity, and that of our allies – human rights; democracy, fundamental freedoms to which every human being is entitled – and we shall use our influence in the world to help confront tyranny, oppression, poverty, conflict and human suffering'.[3]

2.6   Amnesty International welcomes this declaration of intent. However, it is important for the foreign secretary to set out in more detail how the FCO will promote and protect human rights under his stewardship. Although Mr Straw may wish to avoid the pitfalls encountered by his predecessor's reference to an 'ethical dimension', he should stress that promoting respect for human rights is crucial to the national interest and cannot be an optional extra in foreign policy. He should make clear to his civil servants and diplomats that they must regard human rights work as a priority and that the government is ready to be accountable for its work in this area.

Human rights culture in Whitehall

2.7   During the government's first term in office, it launched a number of initiatives to strengthen a commitment to human rights within the foreign office and other departments. Within the FCO, civil servants have spent time working in non-governmental organisations (NGOs) and NGO staff have travelled in the opposite direction. The exchanges helped to generate new ideas and enhanced understanding of the opportunities and constraints of working in the governmental and non-governmental sectors.

2.8   The FCO adopted a more open approach, for example by meeting with NGOs before major human rights events, such as the annual session of the UN Commission on Human Rights (UNCHR) and the Human Dimension meetings of the Organisation for Security and Cooperation in Europe. As under the previous government, new ambassadors were encouraged to seek the views of NGOs before taking up their posts.

2.9   The Human Rights Policy Department enjoyed greater status within the FCO and an increase in staffing. Country desks and the UK's embassies and high commissions (referred to collectively as UK missions) were asked to develop human rights strategies and increase their monitoring of human rights. Amnesty International and other NGOs, media commentators and academic experts contributed to the human rights training programmes initiated under the Conservative administration and maintained by Labour.

2.10   Since April 1998, the FCO has also benefited from the Human Rights Project Fund (HRPF). This currently has an annual budget of £5 million and, according to FCO figures, has provided £15 million to 400 projects in 90 countries since its inception.

2.11   A number of themes have been prioritised for HRPF, including:
• freedom of expression, religion and assembly;
• rule of law co-operation, including prison reform, combating torture and the death penalty;
• promoting the rights of ethnic or minority groups, including displaced people;
• promoting the rights of the vulnerable, including children, women and the disabled;
• human rights awareness and education;
• supporting national human rights institutions.

2.12   Much of the funding is disbursed through UK missions. This is useful in encouraging and supporting embassies and high commissions to develop human rights strategies.

2.13   In Kenya, for example, where torture remains a significant problem, support has been provided, via the UK mission in Nairobi, to the Independent Medico-Legal Unit for its work in treating prisoners and raising awareness of the incidence of torture. In India, the British High Commission sponsored a project to investigate caste violence as experienced by dalit communities and to study the forms of civil society mobilisation against it. In Guatemala, the HRPF has supported the fight against impunity by providing funds for the Truth Commission, for a forensic anthropology team and for the victims seeking justice for past violations.

2.14   In October 2000, the BBC World Service was awarded its largest ever grant, £639,000, to produce a series of programmes explaining the principles embodied in the Universal Declaration of Human Rights to different countries and regions. The FCO estimates that the potential audience for the *I have a right to…* programmes is 125 million.

2.15   Amnesty International believes that the various initiatives have had an impact. While some officials appear to believe that a concern for human rights is marginal to UK interests or is an obstacle to 'friendly relations', others, and indeed whole sections of the FCO, have shown commitment and imagination.

2.16   Beyond the FCO, the department making the most obvious contribution to human rights is the Department for International Development (DFID). The main focus of DFID's work is contribute to the attainment of internationally agreed development targets, in particular to halve the proportion of people living in abject poverty by 2015 and to ensure universal primary education and access to basic health care for all. DFID has championed the 'rights-based approach to development', which is based on the view that economic, social and cultural development is a matter of fundamental human rights, redressing the historical emphasis on civil and political rights.

2.17   In October 2000, DFID published a strategy document entitled *Realising human rights for poor people*. According to this paper, '[a]ll states… regardless of the level of economic development, are to ensure respect for civil, political and subsistence rights for all, while all other economic and social rights must be progressively realised by policies and steps that are deliberate, concrete and targeted'.[4]

2.18   The Ministry of Defence (MoD) also acknowledged that it has a role in the protection of human rights abroad. Following a major 'Strategic Defence Review', the MoD identified a new 'defence diplomacy' mission. This is defined as the use of MoD assets 'to dispel hostility, build and maintain trust and assist in the development of democratically accountable armed forces, thereby making a significant contribution to conflict prevention and resolution'.[5]

2.19   These are positive developments. In contrast, trade minister Richard Caborn told a parliamentary committee in February 2000 that the Department of Trade and Industry (DTI) 'is not responsible for human rights'. The Minister was giving evidence to an inquiry into UK support for a project to construct a dam in Turkey, with potentially very damaging effects on people, international relations and the environment (see box on page 12). Nobody expects the DTI to be the lead department on human rights issues, but it must accept responsibility for the impact of its actions.

Annual reports

2.20   A welcome innovation during the period was the introduction of the FCO's *Human Rights Annual Report*. The initial report in 1998 was useful but provided inadequate information about the department's policies and activities. The 1999 and 2000 reports were improved and Amnesty International commends the FCO's Human Rights Policy Department for consulting about the publication with external parties, including Amnesty International.

2.21   The reports have produced at least three important benefits.
• They explain policies such as 'critical engagement' in more detail than can be contained in the soundbites and speeches of ministers.
• They provide a fuller picture of the FCO's human rights activities. Political and media attention generally focuses on major policy matters, controversies and mistakes. The annual report describes small-scale, low profile but valuable activities that would otherwise be absent from public view.
• They provide a very useful mechanism for scrutinising government action. Amnesty International believes that parliament should use the report as the basis for an annual review of human rights and foreign policy. We note that the foreign affairs committee conducted inquiries into the government's human rights policy in 1999 and 2000 and urge it to continue to do so.

Critical engagement

2.38   'Critical engagement' is the government's policy of choice when dealing with states that violate human rights. The FCO has described it as a rejection of the 'row or kow-tow' approach, allowing the government to raise

The Ilisu dam

2.22   On 21 December 1999, the Secretary of State for Trade and Industry announced that he was 'minded' to grant export credit support for the Ilisu dam project in south-east Turkey. This region is marked by serious human rights abuses in the context of a conflict between the government and Kurdish armed opposition groups.

2.23   His announcement specified four areas to be addressed before the Export Credit Guarantee Department (ECGD) could provide support: a population resettlement programme 'which reflects internationally accepted practice and includes independent monitoring'; measures to maintain upstream water quality; assurances of continued downstream supply; and plans to preserve archaeological heritage.

2.24   Shortly after the secretary of state's announcement, the House of Commons international development select committee launched an inquiry into the ECGD and the Ilisu dam project. This proved to be highly controversial.

2.25   On 1 February 2000, the committee took oral evidence from DTI minister Richard Caborn. One committee member, Ann Clwyd MP, asked him what assessment had been made of the human rights situation in that part of Turkey. The minister replied that the FCO and other departments had been consulted but that there was 'nobody who has come back and raised the human rights question in terms of this dam and the awarding of ECGD cover'.[6]

2.26   On 12 July 2000, the committee published a highly damning report noting that it was 'astonished that the Foreign Office did not raise any questions about the proposed Ilisu Dam and its effect on the human rights of those living in the region'.[7] On the same day, the committee's chairman, Bowen Wells MP, questioned the government's commitment to human rights in a media interview.

2.27   In response, the then FCO minister Keith Vaz wrote to Mr Wells. He suggested that criticism was inaccurate and that 'during 1999 Ministers and officials raised our human rights concerns explicitly in correspondence with the DTI.' He said that Richard Caborn's evidence had been 'misunderstood' and the FCO position 'misrepresented'.[8]

2.28   Bowen Wells was therefore faced with a letter from one minister saying that the FCO had expressed human rights concerns and evidence from another minister suggesting that no such questions had been raised. He therefore wrote to Keith Vaz on 13 July 2000, stating: 'it is now necessary for the Committee to see all correspondence between the FCO and the DTI on the Ilisu Dam to 1 February 2000.'[9]

2.29   In September 2000, the government sent its formal response to the committee. It stated that the 'FCO specifically raised questions about the environment, human rights and the wider range of social and regional issues'. It also stated that Richard Caborn told the committee that the FCO had not raised human rights questions because he thought he was being asked about the dam's regional human rights impact.[10] The response appears contradictory: either the FCO did raise questions about the dam's effect on human rights in the region or it did not.

2.30   When the response was sent to the committee, a

human rights issues while maintaining or even expanding diplomatic, political, commercial and cultural relations.

2.39　Critical engagement may describe the FCO's approach to the majority of its bilateral relationships, with only a few countries, such as Iraq and Myanmar, deemed sufficiently uncooperative for it to be replaced with a policy of isolation and confrontation.

2.40　The potential advantages of the policy are clear. In some countries, the political leadership includes both reforming and reactionary elements. Critical engagement could offer an opportunity to raise concerns in a way that lends support to reformers by, for example, rewarding improvements with increased engagement.

2.41　In other countries, human rights violations may be widespread but the authorities acknowledge the problem. Critical engagement

thus offers a chance to maintain a focus on the challenges while supporting solutions.

2.42　However, while the potential advantages of critical engagement are clear, so are the pitfalls. The policy might be used as a fig leaf for business as usual, allowing political and commercial relationships to be encouraged while paying lip-service to human rights.

2.43　The dangers of critical engagement are reinforced when the UK enters a formal human rights dialogue. In recent years, the government has maintained such formal dialogues with China and Russia, and the FCO seems keen to expand the approach.

2.44　Again, the theory behind the concept is attractive. A human rights dialogue allows senior officials with specific geographic and/or human rights expertise to sit down and discuss a situation, raise concerns, register progress and

---

covering letter from the Secretary of State for Trade and Industry was attached. This notes the committee's request for correspondence and states: 'I hope that the correspondence, combined with this Government Response, clarifies the question of FCO advice.'[11] The letter was dated 19 September 2000, the same day that Keith Vaz apparently refused the committee's request. He subsequently also refused a request for confidential access to the documents. Bowen Wells therefore complained to the parliamentary commissioner for administration (the ombudsman).[12]

2.31　The ombudsman determined that the documents themselves should not be released in order to protect the confidentiality of the decision making process, but could see no reason why the essential elements of the information should not be provided. He therefore summarised the exchanges between the DTI and the FCO.

2.32　After examining this summary, the committee issued a further report. It notes that the material provided by the ombudsman 'appears to confirm the Committee's suspicion that FCO advice on human rights was limited to the issue of resettlement and that it did not extend to the more general issues of human rights and conflict in the region'.[13]

2.33　In its official response to this further report, the government rejected the committee's analysis of the ombudsman's summary. The government's line is highly unconvincing.

2.34　It noted that the summary 'refers to advice being given by the FCO' on policy towards the Kurds and human rights abuses in south-east Turkey.[14] What the ombudsman actually referred to was the FCO's provision of 'brief lines to take in response to correspondence about the project'.[15]

Amnesty International does not consider that advice on how to answer letters is the same as an analysis of the dam's regional human rights impact.

2.35　The government also noted that detailed background on the issue of human rights in Turkey was provided 'in the context of a briefing for the then Minister for Trade's visit to Turkey in May 1999'.[16] Again, this is not the same as a detailed analysis of the dam's impact. However, it should at least have alerted DTI ministers and officials to the general situation. If the FCO failed to provide an assessment of the regional human rights consequences, the DTI should have taken responsibility for clarifying whether this was because of oversight or because the FCO believed there were no such consequences.

2.36　It appears that the FCO did stress the need for a resettlement plan in accordance with international standards. This is to be commended. It also seems clear that the FCO did not provide an analysis of the wider regional human rights impact. This is a serious omission. DTI ministers and the ECGD also deserve criticism for being passive consumers of human rights assessments from other departments rather than pro-active seekers of the fullest possible information.

2.37　In contrast, the international development committee should be congratulated for its tenacity. Amnesty International UK believes that select committees have a duty to scrutinise government departments to assess how they take account of human rights priorities in their deliberations. An understanding of interdepartmental discussions is crucial to making this assessment. Amnesty International therefore notes with concern that the committee lacks the power to scrutinise interdepartmental correspondence.

suggest actions that will bring about improvements.

2.45   The danger is that human rights become pigeon-holed into annual or twice yearly formal meetings between officials, allowing the bulk of the bilateral relationship to pay minimal attention to human rights concerns because they are being tackled elsewhere.

2.46   Any policy must be assessed in terms of its effect on the ground and whether it achieves its objectives within an envisaged timeframe. The success of critical engagement and human rights dialogues also depends on the other government's willingness to talk and ultimately acknowledge that there are problems that must be addressed.

2.47   The foreign affairs committee has called for greater detail and consistency in the FCO's treatment of country situations in its annual human rights report. In response, the government has suggested that 'countries listed might be less willing to engage with the UK in critical dialogue'. This reinforces a perception that critical engagement requires public expressions of concern to be played down. It also highlights the danger of a human rights dialogue becoming its own prisoner, with the UK modifying its actions in response to the explicit or implicit threats of partner countries to terminate a dialogue.

2.48   The government is enthusiastic about human rights dialogues and Amnesty International agrees that they can serve a very useful purpose. However, the dangers are such that the FCO needs to use much clearer criteria for determining when a dialogue might be appropriate and when it is not working. To begin with, a human rights dialogue cannot be sustained with a government that refuses to accept that a problem exists or where discussions are marked by sustained obfuscation. A dialogue must also be based on shared analysis with concrete objectives for change. There must be a reasonable expectation that some if not all improvements on the ground can be achieved within an agreed timeframe. Both sides must be willing to acknowledge the problems publicly and set out the measures intended to address them.

Case studies
China
2.49   The most notable bilateral human rights dialogue is with China. There is also an EU-China dialogue. The approach seemed promising when China signed the International Covenant on Economic, Social and Cultural Rights in 1997 and the International Covenant on Civil and Political Rights (ICCPR) in 1998. Since then the government has claimed other successes for the policy, including visits by various bodies, the establishment of a working group to discuss China's ratification of the ICCPR, and legal exchanges to familiarise the Chinese with the UK's approach to criminal justice and human rights.

2.50   However, while the dialogue has continued, respect for fundamental civil and political rights in China has deteriorated. Amnesty International believes that the UK should take a firmer, public stance on the issues of concern. The FCO describes the dialogue as an opportunity to discuss difficult issues. It is by no means clear, however, that questions receive answers or that the Chinese authorities take the dialogue seriously.

2.51   For example, one of the 'difficult issues' is the death penalty. The FCO has pointed to China's long-term aspiration to end the death penalty. But this aspiration conflicts with the widespread use of capital punishment, the expansion of its scope and the manner of its use. In the latest 'Strike Hard' campaign against crime, at least 2,960 people were sentenced to death and 1,781 executed between April and June 2001. Executions were recorded for a wide range of offences, including bribery, pimping, embezzlement, tax fraud and theft, as well as violent crimes. The Chinese authorities routinely ignore international standards on the use of the death penalty.

2.52   For a number of years, the UK and the EU have sought information from the Chinese authorities, for example, statistics on the number of death sentences passed and executions carried out. To the best of Amnesty International's knowledge, the Chinese government has not provided this data.

2.53   Although the UK government highlights co-operation with China in preparation for its ratification of the ICCPR as an achievement of dialogue, Amnesty International questions Beijing's commitment to the convention. Signature of an international treaty is supposed to indicate that a government supports its objectives. However, political dissidents, labour activists, Falun Gong practitioners and the adherents of other religious or spiritual systems have faced harsh repression and long sentences in recent years.

2.54   In 1998 Prime Minister Tony Blair visited China and spurned opportunities to raise human rights concerns in public. Almost immediately after Mr Blair's visit, the Chinese authorities increased their repression of democracy activists.

2.55   In 1999 Chinese president Jiang Zemin visited the UK. Protests were banned in St James' Park while Jiang was being welcomed and during his procession to Buckingham Palace. Police vans were used to mask demonstrators at other venues and there were attempts to remove protest banners and Tibetan flags from the routes along which president Jiang travelled.

2.56   In response to public criticism and the possibility of legal action by the Free Tibet Campaign, the Metropolitan Police issued two statements. One acknowledged that it was unlawful for officers to remove banners and flags solely on the basis that they were protesting against China. The second statement acknowledged that it would also be unlawful to position vans in front of protesters to suppress free speech. However, the police denied that the positioning of vehicles was intended for this purpose.

2.57   The government denied having influenced the police. Amnesty International is unconvinced by the denial. The actions of the police suggested that there was a policy to shield president Jiang from popular protest. Those actions violated the rights of UK citizens.

2.58   The annual session of the UNCHR is one arena where the UK government's approach to China becomes apparent. Until Labour assumed power, the UK had traditionally supported attempts to introduce a critical resolution on China. In recent years, UK ministers have mentioned the country's human rights situation in their speeches to the commission but have refused to 'co-sponsor' critical motions tabled by the United States.

2.59   The year 2001 saw a minor modification in this approach but only to the extent that EU member states said that they would support a critical US resolution if it survived China's motion that the commission take 'no action'. In previous years, the EU had focused only on this 'no action' motion, suggesting that it was an abuse of the commission's procedures, while remaining silent on the resolution itself.

2.60   The UK has consistently defended its position by highlighting the constant success of the 'no action' motion. According to the government, confrontation is futile and would hand China a diplomatic victory.

2.61   This position is weak. The act of proposing or co-sponsoring a critical resolution would make clear to the UK public and the Chinese government the seriousness with which the UK views the human rights situation in China. China takes considerable effort to dissuade countries from supporting a critical resolution and would therefore be susceptible to a diplomatic defeat even if the resolution ultimately failed.

2.62   One must also ask, if China can claim a victory when a resolution is defeated, how much more complete is that victory when a resolution is not even tabled?

2.63   In March 2001, Robin Cook noted that China had 'engaged more fully at international level on human rights [but] within the domestic arena the record on human rights is grave and even more dissidents are being arrested.' Amnesty International believes that this 'paradox' demands a firmer diplomatic tone towards China, bilaterally and through the EU.

2.64   The UNCHR session in 2002 will be particularly important. It will be the first session following the success of China's Olympic bid. Although the prospect of the Beijing games in 2008 might lead to human rights progress, it is just as likely to send a signal to the Chinese government that it can be fully embraced by the international community even while repression worsens.

2.65   A clear signal in 2002 is therefore necessary. Unless there has been a significant improvement in the human rights situation in China, the UK should urge the EU to sponsor or co-sponsor a resolution criticising human rights violations committed by the Chinese government.

Saudi Arabia

2.66   Gross and systematic human rights violations persist in Saudi Arabia. These include arbitrary arrest, indefinite detention without trial, summary trials, cruel judicial punishments such as amputation and flogging, and frequent use of the death penalty. One of the principal contributory factors is that the criminal justice system is shrouded in secrecy.

2.67   The UK has no formal human rights dialogue with Saudi Arabia. The UK government has traditionally said little if anything about the Saudi government's violation of human rights, reflecting the primacy given to Saudi Arabia's economic, political and strategic importance to the UK.

2.68   The Labour government maintained a largely softly-softly approach but occasionally expressed concerns publicly in parliamentary answers, entries in annual human rights reports and through EU statements at the UNCHR.

2.69   However, there were encouraging developments in Labour's approach. In June 2000, FCO minister Peter Hain did mention human rights at a London conference on investment in Saudi Arabia. It was only a passing mention and carefully phrased. Nevertheless, that human rights were referred to at all in a seminar targeted at businessmen represents a step in the right direction. Human rights have also been a subject of discussion in bilateral meetings.

2.70   In April 2000, Saudi Arabia announced its intention to increase its engagement with the international human rights mechanisms, not least through seeking – and obtaining – election to the UNCHR that year. It also announced that two national human rights bodies would be established, one governmental and one non-governmental. These and other measures suggest the beginnings of a concrete agenda for discussion and action.

2.71   The UK should seize the opportunity to engage Saudi Arabia in a sustained fashion. However, such engagement must be geared to the implementation of real improvements in human rights for all the country's residents. In the absence of such improvements, the UK should, at the very least, push for the UNCHR to consider Saudi Arabia's record.

Iraq

2.72   In certain circumstances, the UK government adopts coercive policies, including economic and military actions. One of the main targets of such policies during the last decade has been Iraq. The UK has been a key supporter of comprehensive economic sanctions imposed by the UN Security Council. British planes patrol 'no-fly' zones over Iraq and have repeatedly engaged in bombing missions, in response to the reported targeting of UK aircraft by the Iraqi military. Amnesty International has expressed concern about the civilian casualties of these missions.

2.73   The economic sanctions have been extremely controversial. Some observers believe that the sanctions have created a humanitarian crisis and two UN humanitarian officials resigned in protest, one in 1998 and one in 2000. Others, including the UK government, contend that the humanitarian problems arise from the actions of the Iraqi government. According to the FCO, the UN's oil-for-food programme is sufficient to meet humanitarian needs.

2.74   Amnesty International agrees with the position adopted by the UN Committee on Economic, Social and Cultural Rights on 8 December 1997 (E/C.12/1997/8). This states that 'inhabitants of a given country do not forfeit their basic economic, social and cultural rights by virtue of any determination that their leaders have violated norms relating to international peace and security.'

2.75   In March 1999 a humanitarian panel reported that 'the gravity of the humanitarian situation of the Iraqi people is indisputable and cannot be overstated'. This is a matter of deep concern.

2.76   Over the past few years, comprehensive sanctions regimes have increasingly been seen as anachronistic. Nonetheless, despite the government's preference for 'smart' or selective sanctions, it maintained the established policy on Iraq for much of its first term of office. During the winter of 2000-2001 however, an apparent willingness to consider a more flexible approach began to emerge in London and Washington.

2.77   On 1 June 2001, the UK and the US proposed a resolution to the UN Security Council that was adopted unanimously as resolution 1352. According to the government, this seeks to achieve two aims. First, to improve the flow of civilian goods to Iraq by restricting the ban to a specified range of goods. Second, to improve controls on the supply of prohibited goods to Iraq. At the time of writing, no agreement had been reached on the detailed implementation of resolution 1352, including the designation of a Goods Review List. Opponents of the sanctions have questioned the sincerity of this new approach.

Russia

2.78   The UK has established a formal human rights dialogue with Russia, the most recent meeting taking place in March 2001. In this context, the UK has raised concerns such as the right to conscientious objection, freedom of expression and religion, prison conditions and prisoners of conscience. From FCO reports, the Russian authorities appear to have a degree of willingness at least to acknowledge the existence of some problems.

2.79   Since September 1999, the dominant human rights issue in Russia has been the conduct of the war in Chechnya. Both sides have been responsible for human rights abuses. Federal security forces have engaged in indiscriminate bombardment of civilian areas and the torture of Chechens in so-called filtration camps.

2.80   The foreign secretary reportedly expressed concerns to his Russian counterpart in November 1999. In the following month, the EU limited its TACIS assistance programme to democracy and rule of law projects. At the same time, the UK sought to intensify contacts with Russia, particularly after the transfer of presidential power from Boris Yeltsin to Vladimir Putin. Prime minister Blair's initial priority appeared to be the establishing of friendly relations with Russia's new leader.

2.81   In March 2000, Mr Blair travelled to St Petersburg and became the first western leader to meet Mr Putin. In April 2000, the Russian president returned the visit. Prior to the London meeting, the prime minister did express concern about Chechnya, albeit in a coded fashion.

2.82   Later that month however, Russia became the first permanent member of the Security Council to be the subject of a critical resolution at the UNCHR, where powerful countries usually escape censure. As well as calling for a halt to hostilities and expressing concern about reports of human rights abuses by both Russian and Chechen forces, the resolution called for a national independent commission of inquiry. Russia did indeed set up investigatory mechanisms but these made little headway, appearing to lack determination, resources and the necessary support from the authorities.

2.83   The UNCHR therefore discussed the issue again in 2001. In his speech to the commission, foreign office minister John Battle spoke of the urgent need for 'a thorough and transparent investigation of widespread allegations of human rights violations in Chechnya. Those responsible must be prosecuted and where appropriate, punished. We...urge rapid progress in bringing to justice those on all sides who have either violated international human rights law or international humanitarian law.'

2.84   In private, diplomats sought to negotiate a draft resolution with which the Russians could agree. With the conflict in Chechnya less intense than in the previous year and holding a much lower media profile, there was considerable pressure to water down the text. Some EU countries were reportedly willing to adopt a more conciliatory stance. In the lead-up to the UNCHR session, there were rumours that the UK was among these. However, Amnesty International UK believes that the government maintained a strong position in Geneva. In the end, consensus could not be achieved and the resolution was adopted by vote with the UK's support.

Zimbabwe

2.85   UK foreign policy towards Zimbabwe is pursued bilaterally and through other fora. The human rights situation in that country has been the subject of massive press coverage in the UK. Many reports have focused on the plight of white farmers, who have been attacked by so-called 'war veterans'. In fact, the attacks on white farmers are part of a broader pattern of human rights violations in a campaign against black and white people who oppose the government, and against the independent media.

2.86   The UK has condemned the violations. For example, at the UNCHR meeting in 2001, Zimbabwe was one of three countries (along with China and Russia) cited in John Battle's speech. He noted the 'campaign of harassment against Zimbabwe's much lauded judiciary, the expulsion of journalists and orchestrated violence against members of the legitimate opposition'.[17]

2.87   The Zimbabwe government has claimed that the UK failed to keep promises to fund land reform measures agreed at Lancaster House in 1980. The UK has responded by professing a willingness to support reform but not in the current climate of human rights abuse and not when land is being distributed to the supporters of president Robert Mugabe.

2.88   At the same time, Zimbabwe's government accuses the UK of neo-colonialism. The UK is therefore keen for other African and Commonwealth countries to express concern about the situation. Progress has been slow however, with the issue of land reform, in particular, finding some resonance on the continent. Zimbabwe is likely to be a high-profile subject for discussion at the Commonwealth summit in October 2001. Human rights violations must be central to those discussions.

Military responses

2.89   In the past four years, UK armed forces have participated in responses to human rights crises in a number of countries, notably in the Yugoslav province of Kosovo, Sierra Leone and East Timor.

Kosovo

2.90   In 1998, after a decade of human rights violations in Kosovo, conflict erupted between state security forces and paramilitaries on the one hand, and the Kosovo Liberation Army (KLA) on the other. Both sides committed abuses although the vast majority of victims were ethnic Albanians. By October 1998, following UN Security Council resolutions and the threat of NATO intervention, the president of Yugoslavia,

Slobodan Milošević, agreed to withdraw forces and allow the deployment of an OSCE verification mission.

2.91   By the beginning of 1999, the cease-fire appeared increasingly fragile, with small-scale KLA attacks being met with excessive force by Serbian police. On 16 January, OSCE monitors entered the village of Račak and discovered the bodies of 45 people. NATO governments responded by intensifying diplomatic pressure on the Yugoslav authorities and renewing threats of military action.

2.92   Following the failure of negotiations at Rambouillet, NATO launched an air campaign on 24 March, with the UK playing a key role. The Yugoslav leadership responded with an upsurge in violence against ethnic Albanians and new offensives against the KLA, with human rights violations being perpetrated mainly by Serbian police and the paramilitaries who operated alongside them. A systematic policy to expel the civilian population began in the first days after the NATO action and hundreds of thousands of people fled to neighbouring countries.

2.93   NATO's air campaign was terminated on 10 June 1999 following the conclusion of an agreement providing for the withdrawal of all federal and Serbian forces and the deployment of the NATO-led Kosovo Force.

2.94   Amnesty International is concerned that during the air campaign NATO forces may have violated the laws and customs of war. Attacks on road and rail bridges and the bombing of a convoy of displaced persons caused significant civilian casualties and brought into question whether NATO was taking sufficient precautionary measures.

2.95   On 23 April, aircraft bombed the headquarters and studios of Serbia's state television and radio, killing at least 16 civilians and wounding another 16. NATO acknowledged that the building was targeted because of its propaganda value to the Yugoslav leadership. Amnesty International believes that this stretches the definition of an objective providing an 'effective contribution to military action' and 'definite military advantage' beyond acceptable bounds of interpretation. Even if the building could properly have been considered a military objective, NATO may have violated the laws of war prohibiting attacks which result in civilian casualties disproportionate to the concrete and direct military advantage anticipated. Broadcasts were resumed three hours after the attack. The Prosecutor of the International Criminal Tribunal for the former Yugoslavia stated that following an examination of the evidence, there was no basis for prosecuting NATO officials.

Sierra Leone

2.96   In July 1999, the Lomé peace agreement apparently brought to an end Sierra Leone's long civil war. Despite extremely serious human rights abuses during the conflict, the peace agreement included an amnesty. Foday Sankoh, leader of the Revolutionary United Front (RUF), an armed opposition group that had committed some of the worst abuses, was appointed vice-president and given a portfolio which included control of the country's gem resources. Amnesty International strongly condemned this impunity clause.

2.97   In October 1999, a UN peacekeeping force, the UN Mission in Sierra Leone (UNAMSIL), was established to oversee implementation of the peace agreement. However, in May 2000 the agreement broke down as the RUF took hundreds of peacekeepers hostage and mounted an offensive, pushing towards Freetown, the capital city.

2.98   The UK government responded quickly. About 600 British soldiers were deployed to evacuate and secure Lungi airport while UNAMSIL received reinforcements. The presence of UK troops and their demonstrable willingness to engage the RUF in combat boosted the morale of pro-government forces and prevented the collapse of the UNAMSIL mission that would almost certainly have led to a human rights crisis.

2.99   Within a few weeks RUF forces were in retreat and by the middle of June the UK's focus switched to training and equipping the Sierra Leone army. Diplomatically, attention switched to initiatives aimed at breaking the link between the illicit trade in diamonds and the supply of weapons and equipment to the RUF. This included public criticism of the role played by Charles Taylor, the president of Liberia.

2.100   In August 2000, the dangers of operating in Sierra Leone were reinforced when a faction known as the West Side Boys, who had previously been allied to government forces, took a number of UK soldiers hostage. In September, the UK deployed troops to rescue the hostages. Although the hostages were saved, 25 West Side Boys were killed along with one British soldier, Bombardier Brad Tinnion.

2.101   The UK's intervention in Sierra Leone almost certainly prevented a human rights catastrophe. However, years of conflict have impoverished the country and destroyed key institutions. For example, Sierra Leone has virtually no functioning criminal justice system.

2.102   Rebuilding Sierra Leone will require sustained commitment and the provision of significant resources by the wider international community. It is crucial that the UK retain a position of leadership in what will be a long haul towards the re-establishment of a stable country that respects and protects the human rights of all its citizens. One of the key challenges will be the establishment of an effective special court to prosecute allegations of human rights crimes and violations of international humanitarian law (see Chapter 3).

East Timor

2.103   For many years, the main aim of successive UK governments was to maintain good relations with the Indonesian government and to cultivate Indonesia as a major market for UK weapons. Indonesian human rights violations were played down, even after Indonesian armed forces used British Hawk jets in East Timor, in breach of the agreement under which they had been supplied.

2.104   In August 1999, the people of East Timor voted overwhelmingly for independence from Indonesia in a ballot organised by the UN. The lead-up to the vote saw outbreaks of violence initiated by anti-independence militias, supported by Indonesian security forces, seeking to intimidate people out of voting for independence. After the ballot, the violence escalated dramatically. Many East Timorese were killed and injured; thousands fled their homes.

2.105   In contrast to its previous record, the UK acted creditably and was among the leading countries pushing Indonesia to act to end the crisis. In mid-September, Indonesia agreed to an international force entering East Timor to protect the civilian population and assist the country's transition to independence. UK soldiers were among the first troops to enter the country.

2.106   As Amnesty International and others have documented, the Indonesian police and military have been implicated in widespread human rights violations against opposition movements in other areas, such as Aceh. The UK government must heed the lesson of East Timor, and prohibit the export of any arms and equipment that might be used for internal repression.

Human rights themes

2.107   The government has given priority to several human rights themes over the past four years. Two are examined below: the death penalty and torture.

The death penalty

2.108   Amnesty International is unconditionally opposed to the death penalty. The organisation rejects as unfounded the claim that capital punishment deters crime and believes that as well as denying the most fundamental right of all, the right to life, capital punishment makes a miscarriage of justice irreversible. Where the death penalty is retained, Amnesty International believes that governments must follow international standards while moving towards a moratorium on executions and eventual abolition. The organisation is pleased that the UK government holds the same position.

2.109   In 1998 parliament abolished capital punishment for the few remaining crimes for which it could still be applied. By December 1999, the government had ratified two treaties seeking the end of the death penalty, the Second Optional Protocol of the International Convention on Civil and Political Rights and Protocol 6 of the European Convention on Human Rights (ECHR).

2.110   The UK's abolitionist steps allowed the FCO to lobby for an end to capital punishment elsewhere in the world and to join other EU member states in establishing guidelines for joint work on capital punishment. In October 1998, the foreign secretary convened a death penalty panel consisting of NGO and academic experts to advise on strategy.

2.111   The UK and EU approach has three basic elements:
• to make opposition to the death penalty clear;
• to make diplomatic representations on individual cases where international standards have not been observed;
• to build and develop international support for abolition of the death penalty.

2.112   This latter element has seen determined lobbying by the EU to secure support for resolutions at the UNCHR calling for an end to capital punishment. In 1999 however, attempts to have the UN General Assembly adopt a resolution were strongly resisted by states that support continued use of the death penalty. There was an impasse and the draft resolution was shelved.

2.113   The USA is one of the priority countries for EU and UK action on the death penalty. This is due to the number of executions carried out in America and because those who are executed include two groups who should be exempt from the penalty – people who are mentally impaired and people who were minors at the time of their crime. The UK has expressed its concern that the USA has made a reservation stating that it would not be bound by Article 6 of the ICCPR, which prohibits imposition of the death penalty for crimes committed by people aged under 18. The UN Human Rights Committee has described the reservation as incompatible with the aims and purpose of the covenant.

2.114   In August 2000, the EU called on then governor George W Bush of Texas to commute the death sentence on Oliver Cruz, who was mentally retarded with an IQ of 64. Despite this intervention, Cruz was executed on 9 August.

2.115   Six months previously, the EU issued a statement welcoming the decision of governor George Ryan to introduce a moratorium on executions in Illinois. The EU said: 'The risk of sentencing innocent individuals to death, as acknowledged by Governor Ryan, is one of the main principles underlying the EU's philosophy concerning the abolition of capital punishment. Therefore, the European Union encourages all states in the US with capital punishment to reflect upon this risk and consider taking a similar measure with a view to the abolition of the death penalty throughout the country.'

2.116   At the Labour Party conference in September 2000, Robin Cook announced his intention to appoint an envoy on the death penalty to reinforce the UK's campaign. So far, no-one has been appointed.

2.117   In February 2001, the FCO announced a change of policy with regard to the imposition of the death penalty on UK nationals. Instead of waiting until judicial processes have been completed, the UK now expresses its opposition to the death penalty whenever it feels representations are appropriate, from the moment that a death sentence becomes a possibility.

Torture

2.118   Torture is banned under international law but persists around the world. Between 1997 and 2000, Amnesty International received reports of torture and ill-treatment by state officials in more than 150 countries. People are tortured not only to extract confessions or information but also because of who they are or what they believe.

2.119   All countries have an obligation to help stamp out torture and in October 1998, Robin Cook used the occasion of an Amnesty International UK festival to announce an anti-

torture initiative by the FCO. This has included, among other things, instructing UK missions to report on torture, banning the export of certain goods (see Chapter 5) and seconding an expert from the World Organisation Against Torture to advise the Human Rights Policy Department on its anti-torture work.

2.120   During the winter of 2000-2001, the UK joined with Denmark to persuade countries that had not done so to ratify the UN Convention against Torture. A number of countries indicated that they were reluctant; some stated an intention to sign and ratify in the near future; others were described as being willing to sign but unable to do so because of difficulties in, for example, passing the necessary domestic legislation.

2.121   In some cases, the response that they 'would if they could' may simply be an excuse. However some small and poor countries may indeed feel that they lack the resources required to legislate for the convention and to implement it effectively by training their judges, lawyers and public authorities. The challenge for the UK and Denmark, perhaps in concert with other countries and institutions, is to follow up their lobbying by providing practical assistance to countries that are willing but not yet able to accede to the convention.

2.122   A further initiative of the FCO's torture campaign was the production of the *Torture Reporting Handbook* by Camille Giffard at Essex University, with a grant provided by the HRPF. The publication guides people who come across incidents of torture to record information in a way that might be useful in future prosecutions. Amnesty International is an enthusiastic user of the handbook. The organisation's staff have taken it on field missions to distribute to non-governmental organisations.

2.123   This year, on 26 June (designated as international day for the victims of torture) the FCO announced the secondment of Detective Chief Inspector Michael Kellet to the secretariat of the European Committee for the Prevention of Torture (ECPT). The ECPT is a body of independent experts who periodically visit detention facilities and conduct spot checks. These lead to the production of reports. DCI Kellet has considerable first-hand knowledge of police systems, procedure and practice. This will help the committee to identify weaknesses in national systems and formulate effective recommendations.

2.124   The UK has also been involved in the development of *Guidelines to EU Policy towards Third Countries on Torture and Other Cruel,*

Inhuman and Degrading Treatment which were agreed in April 2001. Based on the death penalty guidelines, these are intended as an operational tool for use in contacts with other countries and in multilateral fora. The guidelines outline a wide range of possible actions to the undertaken by the EU, its representatives and officials, including:
• supporting international human rights mechanisms and strengthening international standards;
• sending embassy representatives to observe trials where defendants may have been subjected to torture and ill-treatment;
• raising concerns in dialogue with third countries and requesting information regarding allegations of torture and ill-treatment;
• taking action in well-documented individual cases;
• urging third countries to prohibit and condemn torture, and to prevent the use, production and trade of torture equipment;
• providing domestic procedures for complaints, including visiting mechanisms;
• funding projects, including training for personnel in places of detention;
• supporting rehabilitation centres for victims.

2.125   The implementation of the EU death penalty guidelines provides grounds for optimism that the torture guidelines will be a useful tool.

2.126   The UK government has played an important role in putting torture on the agenda of the OSCE by providing funds for the organisation's expert panel on torture. The OSCE's activities have helped to focus increased governmental and non-governmental attention on the problem of torture in Central Asia.

2.127   For the past ten years, the international community has been attempting to create an optional protocol to the Convention Against Torture. This initiative, originated by Costa Rica, aims to create a global system of external inspection of places of detention, as is undertaken by the ECPT.

2.128   An intergovernmental group met to consider the optional protocol in February 2001. At this meeting, Mexico tabled a new proposal in which national mechanisms would have primary responsibility for monitoring in their own countries. This would be a very weak instrument. The UN Committee against Torture and the UN Human Rights Committee have repeatedly questioned the effectiveness of the existing mechanisms. The EU countries agreed that the Mexican draft was unacceptable and tabled their own text as an alternative to Mexico's proposal.

2.129   There is a growing sense that the negotiations on the optional protocol are reaching an impasse. It would be deeply regrettable if the initiative were to be abandoned. However, the understandable desire to seek agreement must not be allowed to drift towards agreement at all costs. A weak optional protocol would be worse than none at all because it would provide a cover of credibility for governments' claims that they are committed to eradicating torture.

The UK and multilateral organisations

The UN Commission on Human Rights

2.130   The major event on the UN's human rights calendar is the annual session of the UNCHR, which takes place over about five weeks each spring. Fifty-three member states have voting rights, although other states and some NGOs can attend and intervene in discussions.

2.131   The structured sessions provide an opportunity to discuss both country and thematic issues and vote on resolutions. The UNCHR can also create new UN special mechanisms, such as special rapporteurs or working groups. It is also central to the development of new human rights treaties.

2.132   On the whole, the UK has played a positive role at the UNCHR. Each year, an FCO minister delivers a speech which usually includes critical references to a number of countries. Peter Hain's statement in 2000 was an exception: he focussed almost exclusively on themes and seemed determined to avoid causing offence.

2.133   This was perhaps because the speech came towards the end of a sustained lobbying campaign by the UK to secure re-election to the commission. Although one might suppose that the UK would have few difficulties in securing its place, the dangers of complacency were illustrated by the USA's failure to gain re-election in 2001.

2.134   While Amnesty International understood the electoral pressures facing the UK at the time of Peter Hain's speech, we regretted its failure to focus on particular countries and were concerned that it might mark a shift towards a weak approach to the UNCHR. John Battle's speech this year was therefore particularly welcome.

The UN Commissioner for Human Rights

2.135   At the UNCHR session in 2001, the UN High Commissioner for Human Rights, Mary Robinson, announced that she would not be seeking re-appointment. She alluded to the difficulties of working within the UN system and suggested that she might be able to do more for human rights from outside the organisation.

2.136   Over recent years, demands on the Office of the High Commissioner for Human Rights (OHCHR) have grown substantially without a parallel increase in resources. Although Mary Robinson was persuaded to remain in post for another year, the problems she encounters demand urgent attention.

2.137   The UK has provided significant voluntary contributions, principally through DFID, for various field missions, capacity building projects and for strengthening the OHCHR itself. However, increased funding from the UN's regular budget is required.

2.138   Robin Cook's comments on 28 March 2001 were therefore welcome. He said: 'Mary Robinson has spoken of her frustration with working in the UN environment. The best way in which we can pay tribute to her record is by carrying through reform of the UN institutions that deal with human rights. A good starting point must be to address what she has said about the need for more secure funding.'[18]

2.139   Mr Cook's statement was supported by John Battle's address to the UNCHR: 'The UK also values the work of the human rights treaty monitoring bodies as a cornerstone of the UN's human rights system. Support for these bodies, and the CHR's mechanisms, as core functions of the High Commissioner's Office, should be priorities for UN regular budget funding.'

2.140   Mr Battle also stated that as a matter of policy the UK government would always agree to requests for visits by special rapporteurs and other mechanisms of the commission and to 'engage constructively' with them. Amnesty International has long urged all countries to issue standing invitations to UN human rights mechanisms and hopes that the UK's commitment will encourage others to make the same pledge.

The Council of Europe

2.141   The Council of Europe is central to human rights protection on the European continent. It is underpinned by the ECHR. As new members have joined the organisation, it has played a major role in developing understanding of and respect for human rights. In particular, it has played the leading role in bringing new entrants towards an abolitionist stance on the death penalty.

2.142   The parliamentary assembly of the Council of Europe, composed of members of national parliaments, was important in keeping the spotlight on human rights violations by Russian forces in Chechnya. Lord Judd led a delegation to the region. To express concern about Russia's failure to respect human rights in the conflict, the parliamentary assembly voted to suspend the voting rights of the Russian delegation.

2.143   A major challenge facing the Council of Europe system is the capacity of the European Court of Human Rights, which hears complaints of violations of the convention. By September 2000, more than 15,000 cases were pending before the court. As observers have noted, the court has been a victim of its own success. In order to address the problem the UK and other member states must provide the court with adequate resources and ensure that any reforms to its operations do not undermine its vital contribution to the protection of human rights.

The Organisation for Security and Cooperation in Europe

2.144   The other major European-wide institution is the OSCE. Its broad mandate includes promotion of security and conflict prevention in the OSCE area, which stretches 'from Vancouver to Vladivostock' and promotion of human rights and civil society, in particular through the organisation's 'human dimension' work.

2.145   As mentioned above, the UK provided funding for the organisation's expert panel on torture. The UK also funded the post of gender advisor in the Office for Democratic Institutions and Human Rights. The gender advisor's brief includes increasing gender awareness, developing the role of women in public life, supporting the advocacy of women's rights and reviewing legislation to aid compliance with international standards, including the Convention on the Elimination of All Forms of Discrimination Against Women.

The Commonwealth

2.146   The principal challenge confronting the Commonwealth when Labour took power in 1997 was the situation in Nigeria. In November 1995, the Commonwealth suspended Nigeria's membership as a response to human rights violations and the failure of General Sani Abacha's military government to make progress on a transitional programme for the restoration of democracy.

2.147   The Commonwealth Heads of Government Meeting (CHOGM) in October 1997 decided to maintain the suspension of Nigeria. In June 1998, Abacha died. His successor, General Abubakar, announced a new transitional timetable. This resulted in presidential elections in February 1999, won by Olusegun Obasanjo. The Commonwealth lifted Nigeria's suspension in May 1999, when President Obasanjo was inaugurated.

2.148   Central to the Commonwealth's scrutiny of Nigeria was the Commonwealth Ministerial Action Group (CMAG). This was established at CHOGM in 1995 to deal with persistent violations of the Harare Declaration, which sets out the principal values of the Commonwealth, including respect for fundamental rights, democracy and rule of law.

2.149   CMAG has focused on unconstitutional changes of government and its scrutiny led to the decisions to suspend the membership of Pakistan in 1999 and Fiji in 2000. CMAG has informally discussed other human rights problems and the UK has argued that its mandate should expand to enable it formally to look at persistent violations of the Harare Declaration. This will be a major challenge for the heads of government in Australia later this year, when they will receive recommendations from a high-level working group on whether and how to expand CMAG's work.

2.150   CMAG has also informally discussed the situation in Zimbabwe on a number of occasions. At a meeting in March 2001, it decided to despatch a ministerial mission to convey the organisation's concerns and to inform the forthcoming CHOGM. However, the Zimbabwe government rejected the mission. A meeting was held in Nigeria instead, where agreement was reached on a land reform process within the law. But there are strong ongoing concerns about the general human rights situation in the country.

The G8

2.151   The G8 comprises the seven leading industrialised countries plus Russia. In 1999, the G8 foreign ministers agreed to make conflict prevention a priority. Focus areas were identified at a further ministerial meeting in Miyazaki in 2000.

2.152   In addition to existing work on small

arms, the G8 undertook to examine such issues as responsibilities of the private sector, children in conflict, mercenaries and private military activity, the illicit trade in commodities such as diamonds and the role of environmental issues in contributing to conflict. At their meeting in Rome in July 2001, G8 foreign ministers decided on two further initiatives in conflict prevention relating to women and corporate citizenship.

2.153   The G8 can undoubtedly provide an opportunity to discuss new ideas and co-ordinate positions but, as yet, it remains unclear whether it is providing added value and effectively supplementing the work of such bodies as the UN and the Organisation for Economic Cooperation and Development (OECD).

2.154   The need for the G8 to demonstrate its effectiveness in fields such as poverty alleviation, conflict prevention and human rights is becoming urgent. Its annual summits have become the focus for massive popular protest, as the latest summit in Genoa in July 2001 once again showed. Concerns about the response of Italian police to the protest in Genoa are outlined below.

The European Union

2.155   The EU is of increasing importance to the UK's foreign policy, including its human rights aspects. The UK's stance is regularly articulated through the declarations and common positions negotiated in the Council of Ministers. At the UNCHR, the EU adopts a common stance and views the maintenance of policy unity between the 15 member states as the overriding priority.

2.156   The advantages are clear. Co-ordinated positions increase the collective diplomatic power of member states and the EU's substantial economic and financial resources can be important assets in support of human rights.

2.157   However, there is a danger, often realised, of weak positions emerging when member states perceive they have economic, political or strategic interests at stake. This leads to the search for an agreed position that is rarely levelled up to the standards of members who place the highest priority on human rights.

2.158   Institutional capacity and working methods further undermine the EU's effectiveness. One of the principal foreign policy innovations of the Treaty of Amsterdam, which came into effect in May 1999, was the creation of the post of high representative and the establishment of a policy planning and early warning unit. These were intended to remedy some of the institutional weaknesses in analysis and policy formulation.

2.159   However, the Policy Planning and Early Warning Unit has not developed a significant capacity to analyse human rights situations and monitor the effectiveness of EU actions. Until and unless this happens, the EU will remain severely constrained in its ability to take the initiative and to develop a forward looking agenda.

2.160   The way in which the EU establishes its priorities also undermines effectiveness in human rights. The country occupying the EU presidency, which rotates every six months, chairs meetings of the Council of Ministers and various council working groups (such as COHOM, the working group on human rights).

2.161   Each country assuming the presidency sets a number of priorities. These can be highly dependent on national priorities and historical ties with former colonies. This leads to inconsistency and discontinuity, whereas in human rights consistency and sustained attention are of crucial importance.

2.162   One example of the need for improved continuity is the EU's approach to the UNCHR. Significant resources are devoted to co-ordinating positions in Geneva and the EU continues actively to promote country resolutions. This is welcome. However, once the discussions in Geneva have been concluded, there appears to be little follow-up of decisions. Amnesty International believes that the UNCHR should be part of a cycle, with the EU paying sustained attention to the observations and recommendations made in the resolutions agreed, in particular those that were proposed or co-sponsored by the EU.

2.163   The EU has sought to increase its transparency in the human rights sphere to some extent. In November 1998, Robin Cook and his German counterpart Joschka Fischer proposed that the EU publish an annual report on its human rights work in other countries. The first such report was published in October 1999.

2.164   The following month saw the first EU-NGO human rights discussion forum, jointly organised by the Finnish presidency and the European Commission. This brought together officials from the various member states, the commission, Members of the European parliament, NGO representatives and academics. One practical result was an invitation for NGOs to participate in one of the regular COHOM meetings.

2.165   While the human rights discussion forum was a welcome initiative, subsequent meetings have raised a concern that they suffer from a lack of focus and continuity. Unless the participants can address these faults, the value will be limited.

Commission communication

2.166   In May 2001, the European Commission published a communication on human rights. This places emphasis on achieving greater 'coherence' of EU policy – coherence being the Euro equivalent of 'joined-up government'. It states an intention to accord human rights a higher priority and to work on them in a more proactive manner.

2.167   It also advocates a more strategic approach for the European Initiative for Democracy and Human Rights, the EU's principal human rights budget line. Four themes will be prioritised:
• democratisation, good governance and the rule of law;
• abolition of the death penalty;
• the fight against torture and impunity and for the international criminal tribunals and the International Criminal Court;
• the fight against racism, xenophobia and discrimination against minorities and indigenous peoples.

2.168   The Council of Ministers responded to the commission communication with its own conclusions in June. These also emphasised consistency, coherence and the importance of 'mainstreaming' human rights. In addition, the council drew attention to the need for openness and dialogue with the European parliament and for the identification and review of priority actions.

2.169   Amnesty International welcomes the commission communication and the conclusions of the Council of Ministers. They represent useful additions to a growing volume of EU texts on human rights. Amnesty International has long called for the council and the commission to make human rights a priority. However, words must be translated into action and unless the EU shows a greater willingness to assert human rights concerns in its relations with other countries, the recent declarations of intent are likely to ring hollow.

Agreements with other countries

2.170   The EU has concluded wide-ranging formal agreements with a significant number of countries. Typically, these include a substantial component on economic, trade and commercial relations but most also establish a political dialogue.

2.171 Since 1992, it has been a requirement that all EU agreements with non-member states must contain a clause stipulating that relations shall be based on respect for human rights.

2.172 However, the EU has failed to take the human rights requirement seriously. It has not adequately assessed the human rights situation in countries with which agreements have been made and does not have the capacity effectively to monitor human rights. It appears that the economic and trade components of agreements take overwhelming precedence over human rights. The UK parliament's foreign affairs committee has raised concerns about the effectiveness of the human rights clause in relation to the EU's Partnership and Cooperation Agreements with countries of the former Soviet Union.

2.173 There have been recent indications that the human rights clause is receiving greater attention. On 3 May, the EU commissioner for external relations, Chris Patten, noted that since its introduction, the clause had led to the suspension of EU agreements with just eight countries: Niger, Tonga, Comoros, Côte d'Ivoire, Tonga, Guinea-Bissau, Fiji and Haiti. None of these countries are either near neighbours of the EU or particularly influential on the world stage.

2.174 Before the commission's communication, Mr Patten suggested that the EU and its Mediterranean partners should set up a group to establish common criteria to make the human rights clause operational. However, Mr Patten's suggestion is unlikely to lead to a substantial change in approach unless it is taken up by the Council of Ministers, which has the primary role in determining the EU's foreign policy.

2.175 Each EU member has to ratify newly-concluded agreements, which gives both the UK government and parliament an opportunity to determine whether human rights considerations have been adequately considered. To date, parliamentary scrutiny of the agreements has been cursory at best. Amnesty International calls upon MPs to review EU agreements carefully before they are ratified and seek firm assurances that the human rights clause will be taken seriously. MPs should note that association agreements have still to be concluded with a number of Mediterranean countries, including Egypt, Jordan, Algeria, Lebanon and Syria.

Monitoring EU members

2.176 The Treaty of the European Union makes it clear that the EU member states must respect human rights and fundamental freedoms, the rule of law and democracy. To prepare for the accession of new member states, the EU has agreed a set of criteria that must be met before candidates can join. Included in the 'Copenhagen criteria' is the political requirement for 'stability of institutions guaranteeing democracy, the rule of law, human rights and respect for and protection of minorities'.

2.177 Thirteen countries are currently applying to become EU members: Bulgaria, Cyprus, the Czech Republic, Estonia, Hungary, Latvia, Lithuania, Malta, Poland, Romania, the Slovak Republic, Slovenia and Turkey. The EU publishes regular reports on the applicants' progress towards meeting the accession criteria. In 2000, the report stated that apart from Turkey, all the applicants met the political criteria, although some still had progress to make in human rights and the protection of minorities. The report drew particular attention to the situation of Roma in some countries. This is starkly illustrated by the continued success of asylum applications in the current member states from Roma citizens of countries aspiring to join the EU.

2.178 As demonstrated by the work of bodies such as the European Court of Human Rights and the European Committee on the Prevention of Torture, the human rights performance of the current EU member states must also be scrutinised constantly. During the recent G8 meeting in Genoa, the response of the police to the protestors gave rise to allegations of brutality and even torture, which the Italian authorities were initially loath to investigate.

2.179 Clearly the use of violence by protestors cannot be condoned and the police have a responsibility to maintain public order. However, if the investigations demonstrate that the police used excessive violence, torture or other cruel, inhuman and degrading treatment, the UK has a responsibility to condemn this as well as the actions of rioters.

2.180 Clarification is also required following reports that UK citizens who were detained were denied access to consular officials. The UK must obtain and make public a response to these allegations, specifying when and how access was requested.

The EU charter

2.181 In June 1999 the EU heads of government decided that 'fundamental principles applicable at European Union level should be consolidated in a charter and thereby made more evident'. A body – called 'the convention' - was established to prepare a draft charter, with representatives of the member states and the European and national parliaments.

2.182   The convention had three key issues to address. First, what rights the charter should enshrine, and in particular whether it should include rights other than those contained in the ECHR. The second issue was whether the charter should be made legally enforceable. The third was whether the EU should accede to the ECHR. The convention was limited to discussion of the first issue. The others were reserved for the EU heads of government.

2.183   From the outset, the UK position was that the charter should be a simple declaration of existing rights defined in international standards and the EU treaties. It should have no legal force. The UK also opposed EU accession to the ECHR.

2.184   The draft charter was completed in October in 2000. In December, the EU's 15 heads of government welcomed the Charter of Fundamental Rights and decided that it should not have any legal force. They also decided that the EU should not accede to the ECHR.

2.185   Although the charter could certainly be improved, Amnesty International believes that it may represent a useful tool to remind member states and EU institutions of their obligations towards their citizens. The European parliament's decision to undertake an annual assessment of the human rights performance of member states against the charter is a welcome development.

2.186   The EU must also acknowledge that human rights concerns exist within the territories of the existing member states. As indicated above, such concerns may grow when new applicants accede. The EU now has a charter describing existing rights in its territory. It must regard this as a starting point towards a comprehensive system of protection based on monitoring EU institutions and member states' performance. The UK also needs to recognise the need for EU institutions to be internationally accountable at a time when their competence in areas directly relating to human rights is expanding. The UK should therefore support the EU's accession to relevant international human rights standards, particularly the ECHR.

Recommendations

The commitment to human rights

■ The foreign secretary should underline his commitment to human rights by setting out his strategy and priorities.

■ The Human Rights Project Fund should be maintained at least at its existing level.

■ The Foreign and Commonwealth Office should continue to prepare a detailed annual report on human rights.

■ The House of Commons foreign affairs committee should continue to conduct an annual inquiry into the government's performance in promoting and protecting human rights.

■ The foreign secretary should publish a detailed statement on 'human rights dialogues', describing among things:
• the criteria for determining that human rights dialogues are appropriate;
• how the objectives for progress and timescales are determined;
• procedures for assessing progress.

■ Each human rights dialogue must be based on:
• shared analysis of problems;
• concrete objectives and a timeframe for their delivery;
• periodic assessments of progress;
• transparency and a willingness to acknowledge problems publicly and in multilateral fora such as the UNCHR.

The death penalty

■ The foreign secretary should appoint an envoy on the death penalty as soon as possible.

Stopping torture

■ The UK government should continue to advocate that the proposed optional protocol to the UN Convention Against Torture must provide for an effective, independent inspection system.

■ The UK and Denmark, possibly together with other states, should follow up their global lobbying initiative by exploring practical ways to help countries that are willing but not yet able to ratify the Convention Against Torture.

The UN Commissioner for Human Rights

■ The UK government should initiate or support initiatives to ensure that the Office of the High Commissioner for Human Rights has adequate and secure funding from the UN regular budget.

The Commonwealth

■ At the heads of government meeting in October 2001, Commonwealth leaders should discuss ways of monitoring and promoting respect for the Harare Declaration and international human rights standards. Human rights must be central to any discussion of Zimbabwe.

The European Union

■ The UK government should propose or support measures to improve the human rights analysis capacity of the EU's policy planning and early warning unit.

■ The UK should take a lead in measures to improve the effectiveness of the human rights clause in EU agreements with third countries.

■ The UK parliament should closely review all proposed agreements with third countries before they are ratified and seek firm assurances that the human rights clause will be taken seriously.

■ The UK government should support the EU's accession to the European Convention on Human Rights.

3 International justice

3.1   Some crimes are so serious that they are regarded as international crimes. Genocide, war crimes and crimes against humanity are, in the words of one international treaty, 'the most serious crimes of concern to the international community as a whole' and as such 'must not go unpunished'.[1]

3.2   However, except for the prosecution of people for crimes committed during World War II, justice has been rare for the victims of such crimes. People have planned and committed systematic violations human rights safe in the knowledge that they could do so with almost certain impunity.

3.3   International justice began to take effect again in May 1993, when the UN Security Council decided to establish the International Criminal Tribunal for the former Yugoslavia (ICTY). Eighteen months later, the Security Council set up another international tribunal in response to the genocide in Rwanda – the International Criminal Tribunal for Rwanda (ICTR).

3.4   These moves added momentum to the campaign to create a permanent international court to try individuals accused of the worst human rights violations. However, in May 1997, as the Labour government embarked on its first term in office, the cynical view largely prevailed that international justice was toothless.

3.5   Most of the people indicted by the ICTY were still at large, while the ICTR had failed to conclude a single trial, despite having suspects in custody. Although negotiations for an international criminal court were well under way, it was a matter of debate whether they could produce an institution with the required independence and strength.

3.6   Today much remains to be done, but the picture in 2001 is different from that in 1997. The ICTY and ICTR are now functioning judicial institutions. A statute for an effective International Criminal Court (ICC) has been agreed and the court is well on the way to becoming a reality. In addition, national courts have shown an increased willingness to bring human rights criminals to justice, including former heads of state and government.

3.7   Through diplomacy, resources and legislation, the Labour government has helped to make international justice more of a reality. A previous Conservative administration also deserves credit for incorporating the UN Convention Against Torture into domestic law, as do the judges who applied its terms to the Pinochet case. Other governments have also been forceful and effective advocates for the international tribunals and for a permanent international criminal court.

The Pinochet case

3.8   Augusto Pinochet assumed power in Chile following a military coup in 1973. Thousands of people were tortured, killed or 'disappeared' by the security forces under his command.

3.9   Pinochet was arrested in London in October 1998, on an official request from a Spanish investigating judge alleging serious crimes committed during the years of military rule. Belgium, France and Switzerland subsequently joined Spain in seeking his extradition from the UK.

3.10   Pinochet contested the extradition and the high court upheld his claim that as a head of state when the crimes were allegedly committed, he benefited from what is known as state immunity. The high court decision was appealed to the House of Lords, which eventually confirmed on 24 March 1999 that state immunity did not apply. The House of Lords decision was one of the most important developments in international criminal law since the Nuremberg trials. It was the first legal ruling to uphold international restrictions on state immunity.

3.11   In April home secretary Jack Straw issued authority to proceed and in October 1999 a court ordered Pinochet's extradition to Spain on charges of torture and conspiracy to torture. There was significant public support for extradition. The home secretary informed parliament that of 70,000 public letters and emails he received, almost all called for Pinochet's extradition.

Fitness for trial

3.12   Shortly after the court ordered the extradition, the government of Chile made representations suggesting that Pinochet was in poor health and unfit to stand trial.

3.13   In response, the home secretary appointed a panel of medical experts to examine Pinochet. In January 2000, Mr Straw stated that 'the unequivocal and unanimous conclusion of the four medical experts was that he is at present unfit to stand trial, and that no change to that position can be expected'. He suggested that he was 'minded' to stop the extradition proceedings. He invited submissions from the states requesting extradition and other interested parties, but without disclosing the medical report to them.

3.14   During the controversy surrounding the medical examination, Professor Sir John Grimley Evans, one of the examining medical experts, was reported as saying that 'all we did was to list the medical facts. Whether those medical facts constitute unequivocal grounds for decreeing unfitness for trial is outside our field of competence and outside our responsibilities'.[2] This differed somewhat from Mr Straw's statement in parliament that '[t]he unequivocal and unanimous conclusion of the three medical practitioners and the consultant neuropsychologist was that... [Senator Pinochet] is at present unfit to stand trial, and that no change to that position can be expected'.[3]

3.15   Amnesty International, other non-governmental organisations (NGOs) and Belgium initiated legal proceedings, arguing that the home secretary's refusal to permit them to see the medical report was unfair.

3.16   In February 2000, the high court agreed, and ordered the home secretary to disclose the medical report to the states seeking Pinochet's extradition and provide them with the opportunity to comment. However, although they voiced reservations, Mr Straw determined that Pinochet was unfit for trial and, in March 2000, decided to halt extradition proceedings and allow him to fly home.

Subsequent events in Chile

3.17   The Pinochet case in the UK encouraged groups and individuals campaigning in Chile for the investigation and prosecution of human rights violations committed during the years of military rule.

3.18   At the time of his arrest in London, Augusto Pinochet enjoyed domestic immunity by virtue of the 1978 amnesty law (described by the Inter-American Commission on Human Rights as incompatible with Chile's international obligations) and his status as senator for life. On his return from the UK, a number of lawyers initiated legal proceedings over cases of 'disappearance' arising from the 'Caravan of Death' military operation. In August 2000 the Chilean supreme court upheld a decision to strip Pinochet of his parliamentary immunity in these cases. However, as in the UK, Pinochet's health appears to have prevented further legal proceedings. In July 2001, the Santiago court of appeals decided to suspend all charges against him, as he was deemed unfit to stand trial.

3.19   Nevertheless, relatives of the thousands of victims of human rights violations committed under military rule continue their quest for truth and justice. Amnesty International hopes that investigations and judicial proceedings against other alleged perpetrators will continue, free from any political interference.

The international criminal tribunals

3.20   The ICTY, based in The Hague, was established by UN Security Council resolution 827 in May 1993 as a response to the widespread violations of international human rights law and international humanitarian law that accompanied the break-up of the former Yugoslavia from 1991.

3.21   The ICTR, based in Arusha, was established by resolution 955 in November 1994 following the genocide that cost up to a million lives in the six months from April 1994.

3.22   Both tribunals have experienced difficulties since their creation and they continue to face significant challenges. However, they have established their credibility.

3.23   By 15 August 2001, the ICTY had publicly indicted 106 individuals (additional 'sealed' or confidential indictments may also have been issued). Of these,
• 18 had seen all charges dropped and indictments withdrawn;
• nine had died (two died in custody, one by suicide);
• five had been convicted and were serving sentences;
• a further 12 were appealing their conviction;
• two had been acquitted;
• 27 indictees remain at large, including Radovan Karadžić and Ratko Mladić, the political and

military leaders of the Bosnian Serb forces.

3.24 In May 1999, the ICTY issued an indictment against the then president of Yugoslavia, Slobodan Milošević and four other senior figures, in connection with violations of human rights and humanitarian law in Kosovo. Milošević thus became the first serving head of state to be indicted for war crimes and crimes against humanity. In June 2001, the Yugoslav authorities surrendered him to the ICTY, where he now awaits trial.

3.25 By August 2001, six people were serving sentences following conviction by the ICTR and a further two cases were subject to appeal. Forty-three individuals were in detention, either on trial or awaiting the commencement of proceedings.

3.26 In October 2000, the ICTR's appeals chamber upheld the conviction for genocide of Jean Kambanda, former prime minister of Rwanda, and his sentence of life imprisonment. Kambanda was the first former head of government to be convicted and punished for genocide.

UK support for the tribunals

3.27 The Conservative government of 1992-97 used the UK's seat on the UN Security Council to help establish both international tribunals and provide them with adequate powers and independence. Since then, and under the Labour government, the UK has developed a strong track record of supporting the tribunals through the provision of staff and resources, assistance with witness protection, provision of evidence, and the apprehension of suspects.

Arrests

3.28 When the international tribunals were established, many doubted that the indicted would ever face trial. In 1997, most indictees were still at large. Today, most are in custody.

3.29 The changes of government in Croatia and the Federal Republic of Yugoslavia have contributed to this success, as has the growing credibility of the ICTY itself. However, the UK government has also played an important role.

3.30 In July 1997, British troops serving with the Stabilisation Force (SFOR) in Bosnia moved to arrest Simo Drljača and Milan Kovačević, indicted for crimes committed in Bosnia in 1992. Drljača was shot dead by UK troops during an exchange of gunfire. Kovačević was arrested, but died of natural causes while in detention.

3.31 The July 1997 arrests demonstrated a more robust approach by SFOR and a renewed

international commitment to the tribunals. The Ministry of Defence reported that, by September 2000, SFOR had carried out 23 detention operations. Thirteen of these occurred in what was then the UK-led sector, with UK troops playing either a direct or a supporting role.[4]

Provision of evidence

3.32 The UK has supplied evidence directly to the ICTY through eye-witness statements from its troops and the provision of evidentiary material in its possession, including intelligence material. In April 1999, the Foreign and Commonwealth Office (FCO) appointed an official to facilitate the provision of such material to the ICTY Prosecutor.

3.33 UK assets have also been used for aerial and ground surveillance of mass grave sites, and personnel have been dispatched to assist the ICTY in the forensic investigation of atrocity sites.

3.34 Witness testimony is obviously crucial to any trial. However, in post-conflict societies the safety of witnesses is a paramount concern. It is therefore particularly welcome that the UK was the first country to sign a witness protection agreement with ICTY.

Finance and resources

3.35 The international tribunals are financed through assessed contributions from UN member states, including the UK. Since 1997, in addition to its assessed contribution, the UK has seconded staff to the tribunals and provided voluntary financial assistance, most notably £1.22 million for the ICTY's exhumations programme and £300,000 to finance an additional courtroom in The Hague. The Department for International Development has sponsored visits of Rwandese magistrates, social workers and NGOs to see justice in progress at the ICTR.

Support for other tribunals

3.36 Since the establishment of the international tribunals for the former Yugoslavia and Rwanda, there have been calls for similar responses to widespread and systematic human rights violations, past and present.

3.37 In Sierra Leone, following the breakdown of the Lomé peace process in May 2000, there were demands to ensure that the perpetrators of human rights abuses should be brought to justice. A feature of the Lomé agreement had been the amnesty offered to all parties for some of the worst crimes seen in any conflict. In June 2000 president Ahmad Tejan Kabbah wrote to the UN secretary-general requesting assistance and guidance for the establishment of a special court to try leading members of the armed opposition Revolutionary

Tharcisse Muvunyi

3.40   In March 1998, Tharcisse Muvunyi was admitted to the UK and granted leave to remain until 12 May 2002. At the time, the UK authorities were unaware of his alleged role in the 1994 genocide as a lieutenant colonel in the Rwandese army.

3.41   However, by December 1998, Muvunyi's identity and presence in London were known. In February and again in November 1999, the government of Rwanda raised his presence in London with FCO ministers and officials. Jenny Tonge, a Liberal Democrat MP, asked what plans the government had to investigate Muvunyi. In a written answer to parliament on 24 November 1999, the foreign office minister, Peter Hain MP, said '[i]t is the responsibility of the International Criminal Tribunal for Rwanda to investigate the allegations of genocide which have been made against Lt Colonel Muvunyi. We are working closely with the tribunal on this'.[5]

3.42   The Home Office helped the ICTR to approach Muvunyi for an interview. However the UK was unable to transfer him to Arusha until the tribunal had made a formal request on the basis of an indictment. Nor could the UK extradite Muvunyi to Rwanda, because the two countries did not have an extradition treaty.

3.43   On 5 February 2000 the Metropolitan Police arrested Muvunyi following a request from the ICTR and, after legal argument, he was transferred to Arusha in October. The following month, he pleaded not guilty to counts of genocide, incitement to commit genocide and crimes against humanity, including rape.

3.44   That Muvunyi could stay in a London suburb for two years before his arrest demonstrated a weakness in UK law and showed how the country could become a safe haven for war crimes suspects. It is believed that the Genocide Act does not cover genocide committed abroad by foreign nationals and it has never been tested. The International Criminal Court Act 2001 remedies some of the weaknesses that became apparent between 1998 and 2000.

United Front.

3.38   The UK played a leading role in gaining support for the proposal. In October, a draft statute for the court was presented to the UN Security Council. However, in April 2001, the Security Council decided that the special court should be funded entirely by voluntary contributions rather than from UN assessments, despite the warnings of the UN secretary-general that this would be 'neither viable nor sustainable'.

3.39   At the time of writing, a budget for the court had not yet been agreed and it remained unclear whether the funds allocated would be adequate for an effective tribunal. Even when a budget is agreed, it is by no means certain that the international community will respond quickly with sufficient pledges to enable the court to begin operations in the near future.

The International Criminal Court

3.45   The idea of a permanent international criminal court was first floated in the aftermath of World War II, but was soon buried by superpower rivalry. It resurfaced after the end of the Cold War. The events in former Yugoslavia and Rwanda, and the establishment of the two ad hoc international tribunals, gave impetus to the campaign for a permanent criminal court.

3.46   The Rome Statute for an International Criminal Court was agreed in July 1998. The ICC will be set up once 60 countries have ratified the Rome statute. At the end of July 2001, 37 countries had done so. By 31 December 2000, the last date that a country could add its signature, 139 countries had signed the statute – indicating support in principle, without ratifying the treaty.

3.47   The ICC will have jurisdiction over genocide, war crimes and crimes against humanity. Eventually, it will also have jurisdiction over a crime of aggression, if the international community can agree on a definition.

3.48   The ICC represents a significant step forward in the fight to end impunity for perpetrators of the worst crimes. Its presence will act as a deterrent to potential human rights violators. ICC proceedings will also help reconciliation by exposing the truth and attaching criminal responsibility to individuals, rather than to entire groups.

3.49   The Rome statute is already encouraging states to pass domestic laws criminalising the 'ICC offences'. Because the ICC is underpinned by the concept of 'complementarity', the primary duty to bring people to justice lies with individual states. The ICC will be able to step in only when states prove unwilling or unable to mount a genuine investigation or prosecution of a suspect.

The Rome conference

3.50   The Rome statute was adopted on 17 July 1998 at the end of a five-week diplomatic conference that was the culmination of years of preparatory negotiations. To facilitate the broadest possible involvement of the international community, the UK contributed to a UN trust fund established to help the poorest countries attend such meetings. The UK also provided financial support to the international NGO Coalition for an International Criminal Court.

3.51   Immediately after taking office, the Labour government actively supported the establishment of an effective international criminal court. In the lead-up to the Rome conference, the FCO encouraged other states to agree a strong statute.

3.52   Most significantly, the UK was the first and only member of the UN Security Council to join the 'like-minded group' of countries who were most in favour of an independent and effective ICC. The relationship between the ICC and the Security Council was one of the most controversial subjects discussed at Rome. Joining the 'like-minded group' meant taking positions different from those other Security Council members, not least key allies such as the USA and France.

3.53   UK support was important in ensuring independent powers of investigation for the ICC Prosecutor, in ensuring that the court could have jurisdiction over war crimes occurring in internal as well as international armed conflict, and in providing for reparations to victims. The UK government also contributed to the inclusion in the statute of sexual crimes such as rape, forced prostitution, forced pregnancy and sexual slavery.

Legislation to permit ratification

3.54   Once the Rome statute was agreed, the UK government announced that it intended to be a founder member of the ICC. To achieve this goal, the UK needs to be one of the first 60 countries to ratify the statute – and in order to ratify, two pieces of legislation are required, for the UK (Westminster) and Scotland.

3.55   The legislation to ratify must ensure that obligations to the ICC are included in domestic law and provide the authorities with the necessary powers to cooperate with the court. The domestic criminalisation of the ICC offences is also necessary if the UK is to incorporate the principle of complementarity.

3.56   Two parliamentary sessions elapsed without the introduction of legislation. However, in August 2000, the FCO published a draft bill for consultation. In December, a bill was introduced in parliament, eventually receiving royal assent on 11 May 2001, the last day of parliamentary business before the general election. Amnesty International urges the secretary of state to make an order to bring the act into force at the earliest opportunity.

3.57   The act contains both strengths and weaknesses. Certainly the government went beyond the minimal requirements of the Rome statute and complementarity. For example, it included provisions to allow those convicted by the ICC to serve their sentence in UK prisons. Nevertheless, the weaknesses are significant.

Immunity of state officials

3.58   Section 23 of the International Criminal Court Act provides for the transfer to the ICC, on request, of persons claiming diplomatic or state immunity. The flaws in this section are the most serious in the act and the only ones to suggest that the UK might fail to honour its obligations under the Rome statute.

3.59   The ICC will have jurisdiction over offences committed on the territory of states that have ratified the Rome statute ('states parties'). The statute makes it clear that once states are party to the agreement, the diplomatic, state and other immunities of its officials cannot bar the prosecution of the latter before the ICC. However, it also acknowledges that the statute cannot override international agreements between states that have ratified the statute and those that have not. This means that the UK is not obliged to surrender a person who has state, diplomatic or other immunity in a country that has not ratified the Rome statute.

3.60   In the UK legislation, subsection (1) of section 23 affirms that proceedings can be taken to transfer individuals to the ICC even if they enjoy state or diplomatic immunity by reason of a connection to a state party. Subsection (2) affirms that proceedings may go ahead even if the defendant can claim immunity because of a connection to a non-state party, provided that country waives the immunities. However, subsection (4) states: 'The Secretary of State may in any particular case, after consultation with the ICC and the state concerned, direct that proceedings (or further proceedings) under this part which, but for subsection (1) or (2), would be prevented by state or diplomatic immunity attaching to a person shall not be taken against that person.'

3.61   This means that the secretary of state may, in any particular case, respect a person's state or diplomatic immunity and order that no proceedings be taken to transfer them to the ICC. This could apply even if immunity has been waived by the country that originally conferred it.

3.62   This is an unacceptable degree of discretion for a secretary of state to exercise without recourse to either domestic courts or parliament, and after mere 'consultation' with the ICC. During the parliamentary process, several peers and MPs raised this issue. Throughout, government ministers could respond only by saying that the clause was there to cope with unforeseen circumstances.

Jurisdiction of UK courts

3.63   The government's draft ICC bill proposed that domestic courts should have jurisdiction over ICC offences that are:
• committed in England, Wales and Northern Ireland;
• committed by a UK national or a person subject to the jurisdiction of UK armed forces.

3.64   NGOs, lawyers and academics pointed out that this meant that the UK could become a safe haven for the perpetrators of genocide, crimes against humanity or war crimes. Many suggested that the bill incorporate a form of 'universal jurisdiction' to permit UK courts to try people present in the UK regardless of their nationality or where the crimes were committed.

3.65   The government introduced its legislation to the House of Lords without changing this aspect of the bill. The prospect of the UK becoming a safe haven for war criminals aroused considerable concern in the House of Lords. In response to pressure, the government amended the bill to bring UK residents within the scope of the law. This was a significant concession and prevents the UK becoming a safe haven for human rights violators who have been granted permanent residence.

3.66   However, no guidance is provided as to the legal meaning of the term 'resident'. It is a rare concept in criminal law and in other areas of law different definitions are applied. For the purposes of the ICC act, courts will have discretion to determine whether someone is a resident. Given the gravity of the ICC offences, it is possible that courts will take a restrictive view.

3.67   The practical implication of the residence test is that while a human rights criminal may not permanently live in the UK with impunity, such a person could visit the country, perhaps for extended periods, perhaps repeatedly, without worrying about either the prospect of domestic prosecution or surrender to the ICC.

3.68   The government used a number of arguments to justify the 'residence' test as opposed to a 'presence' test:
• *If a person was found in this country but was not a resident, he or she would be surrendered to the ICC.* However, the ICC will not have jurisdiction over crimes committed on the territory of non-state parties by their nationals. Moreover, even where the ICC is able to exercise jurisdiction it may choose not to. This might be, for example, because resource constraints have led it to pursue only the very worst crimes or the most senior offenders.
• *A suspect could be extradited to a third country.* However, this requires, first, a third country's willingness to seek extradition. Second, it requires that the UK and the third country have an extradition treaty covering the crimes in question. Third, the government would have to be satisfied that there was no risk of torture or capital punishment if the extradition went ahead. All three conditions may not always be present.
• *It is established policy for the government not to adopt universal jurisdiction unless specifically required to by an international treaty.* This may reflect policy but it does not deal with the merits of the issue. Genocide, crimes against humanity and war crimes are exceptional offences. Amnesty International believes that a policy change would be preferable to the prospect of the perpetrators of such offences visiting the UK with impunity.

3.69   Despite the government's concession, the issue carried over into the House of Commons' consideration of the bill. Although there was support from all benches for broadening jurisdiction to include those present in the UK, the imminent general election reduced the room for manoeuvre. Had MPs amended the bill, parliamentary procedure would have demanded its return to the House of Lords. The choice presented by the government was to accept the bill as it stood or to lose it until the next parliament. In consequence the ICC act retained the residence test.

Compensation and rehabilitation support for victims

3.70   The UK helped to ensure that the Rome statute provided for compensation and reparations. Those convicted by the ICC may be ordered to pay fines. Recognising the difficulty in enforcing such orders and the fact that many of those who appear before the court may have only meagre assets, the statute also provides for the establishment of a trust fund for victims.

3.71   Amnesty International believes that this

leaves an important issue outstanding. Those who come before UK courts for ICC offences may have very limited assets. Even where assets are substantial, their recovery may take a long time, or may prove impossible. It is therefore desirable to provide for the payment of compensation or support to victims from a fund. Many of the victims of ICC offences tried in UK courts will be foreign nationals, possibly living in countries whose government, economy and social infrastructure has been destroyed by conflict. However, Amnesty International is not aware of any existing source of support for the victims of violent crime committed abroad but prosecuted in this country.

The International Criminal Court (Scotland) Bill

3.72   Although the Westminster parliament has now passed the International Criminal Court Act, the UK cannot ratify the Rome statute until the Scottish parliament passes its own legislation.

3.73   The ICC (Scotland) bill began its passage through Holyrood in April 2001 and may be passed in the autumn. The Scottish parliament cannot remedy the problems inherent in section 23 of the Westminster Act, since it applies to the whole UK.

3.74   However, members of the Scottish parliament do have the opportunity to ensure that Scottish courts have the power to prosecute any person present in Scotland, thus ensuring that Edinburgh and the Highlands are crossed off the holiday destination list for war crimes suspects. The Scottish parliament can also create or identify a fund to support or compensate victims when a convicted person's assets are negligible or irrecoverable.

Challenges for Labour's second term

Support the fight against impunity in national courts

3.75   The Pinochet case encouraged victims, lawyers and human rights groups campaigning to bring to justice those responsible for human rights violations. Since 1998 Senegal, Mexico, Italy, Guatemala, Spain, Haiti and other countries have seen legal proceedings to secure the extradition or trial of heads of government and officials suspected of torture and other crimes.

3.76   Not all attempts to end impunity succeeded. However, they merit the support of the UK government, whether in the form of financial help to groups seeking to bring cases to court or, perhaps more important, in the form of political support.

3.77   Many of the individuals seeking to bring human rights violators to justice show great courage in the face of intimidation, harassment and threats to their lives. The government should support the fight against impunity, through international institutions and bilaterally. This will not only demonstrate the UK's commitment to justice, but also encourage those leading the struggle against impunity.

Support for the international tribunals

3.78   The UK has a strong track record of support for the Hague and Arusha tribunals and has played an important role in securing international agreement for a special court in Sierra Leone. Continued financial, diplomatic and practical support is essential.

3.79   The president of the ICTY, Claude Jorda, has indicated that unless its working methods are reformed, the tribunal is unlikely to complete its task until the middle of the next decade. Following a visit to the ICTR in June 2000, a Law Society delegation painted a picture of a tribunal struggling with institutional weaknesses and inadequate resources.[6]

3.80   The UK should therefore continue to support the reform and financing of these tribunals, and continue to provide intelligence material and other assistance with the gathering of evidence.

3.81   The proposed special court for Sierra Leone also requires the UK's active engagement. The Security Council's decision to fund the court through voluntary contributions was regrettable. The UK government should contribute, and seek to persuade other governments to contribute, sufficient money to enable the special court to perform effectively.

Support for the ICC

3.82   If the Scottish parliament passes the ICC (Scotland) Act in the autumn, the government should achieve its goal of becoming a founder member of the ICC.

3.83   Once the UK has ratified the Rome statute it must continue to encourage other countries to ratify it. This will require the government to show international leadership and to stand up to the court's opponents.

3.84   This may be particularly important given that the US government has refused to ratify the treaty and some US politicians are urging action to dissuade other countries from ratifying. As Bill Pace, convenor of the NGO Coalition for an International Criminal Court, has said, '[t]he question is whether the Bush administration assumes an attitude of benign neglect, or whether it will be engaged in it, or oppose it'.[7]

3.85   The prime minister and foreign secretary should seek to dissuade president George W Bush from taking the path of opposition and continue to persuade American politicians that the ICC has sufficient safeguards to address their fears. Should these efforts fail, however, the UK, with its EU partners, must ensure that it is as enthusiastic and vociferous in campaigning for the ICC as other countries might be in opposing it. The EU common position on the ICC, agreed on 11 June 2001, and the EU-Canada joint statement of 21 June provide encouragement in this regard.

3.86   Even if the USA and others do actively campaign against the ICC, the court is likely to become a reality within the next two years, requiring the commitment of its member states. The UK will need to:
• ensure that the ICC is adequately resourced;
• assist the court by providing evidence, including intelligence information;
• arrest and transfer any individuals requested by the ICC, without applying section 23(4) of the ICC act;
• pro-actively investigate suspects falling under the jurisdiction of UK courts and seek their prosecution, seeking the broadest possible interpretation of 'resident';
• support the ICC's independence, in particular by using its position on the Security Council to prevent that body arbitrarily obstructing ICC investigations and prosecutions.

3.87   Finally, the government should look again at the International Criminal Court Act 2001, with a view to amending section 23, to provide for domestic jurisdiction over all persons present in the UK and to ensure that the victims of ICC offences tried in the UK can receive compensation or support if the perpetrators are unable to pay. The Scottish Executive and MSPs should introduce these amendments into the Scottish bill.

Recommendations

■ The government should continue to provide financial, diplomatic and practical support for the ICTY and the ICTR.

■ The government should contribute, and seek to persuade other governments to contribute, sufficient money to enable the proposed special court for Sierra Leone to perform effectively.

■ The government, bilaterally and through the EU, should continue to encourage other countries to ratify the treaty to establish the International Criminal Court.

■ If the ICC is established, as appears likely, the UK government should make every effort to.
• ensure that the ICC is adequately resourced;
• assist the court by providing evidence, including intelligence information;
• arrest and transfer any individuals requested by the ICC, without recognising any state or diplomatic immunity under section 23(4) of the ICC act;
• investigate suspects falling under the jurisdiction of UK courts and seek their prosecution, seeking the broadest possible interpretation of 'resident';
• support the ICC's independence, in particular by using its position on the Security Council to prevent that body arbitrarily obstructing ICC investigations and prosecutions.

■ The secretary of state should make an order to bring the International Criminal Court Act 2001 into force at the earliest opportunity.

■ The UK government should amend the International Criminal Court Act 2001
• to provide for domestic jurisdiction over all persons present in the UK;
• to ensure that the victims of ICC offences tried in the UK can receive compensation or support if the perpetrators are unable to pay.
The Scottish Executive and MSPs should introduce these amendments into the Scottish bill.

4　Asylum policy

The early years: the 1998 white paper and the 1999 bill

4.1　The election of the Labour government in 1997 held out the promise of a fresh approach to UK asylum policy. The preceding decade had seen a stream of legislative and procedural measures whose cumulative effect had been seriously to undermine the quality of protection afforded by the UK to the world's refugees. It was, moreover, widely recognised that the administration of the UK's asylum procedures was a shambles.

4.2　Initial indications were encouraging. Shortly after the general election, the Home Office announced that it would review all aspects of immigration and asylum policy and practice. The initial phase of the review, which included public consultation exercises, culminated in the publication in July 1998 of the white paper *Fairer, Faster and Firmer – A Modern Approach to Immigration and Asylum.*

4.3　The white paper's analysis of the problem contained much that Amnesty International and other commentators were happy to endorse. The failings identified in the immigration and asylum system included delays and backlogs, high costs, inadequate resources, outdated and complex procedures, and a piecemeal approach to the development of policy and practice.

4.4　The solutions that were proposed to address these problems were somewhat less welcome. True, the package included some important progressive elements: a limited administrative 'amnesty' for thousands of applicants who had been waiting several years for a decision on their claim, for example; and the proposal for a regulatory scheme to control unscrupulous immigration 'advisers' or 'consultants'.

4.5　Regrettably, however, these positive aspects were greatly outweighed by proposals which, at best, failed to address existing problems; and, at worst, continued the established trend of curtailing the rights of people attempting to seek refuge in the UK. These proposals, which were either implemented directly, or otherwise carried forward into the Bill which became the Immigration and Asylum Act 1999, included (to cite just two examples):

4.6　*Pre-entry controls.* These controls – designed to prevent asylum seekers gaining access to the UK – are a well-established element of immigration and asylum policy. The imposition of visa regimes on nationals of the main 'refugee-producing' countries; carrier sanctions which require employees of airlines and other private companies to take on immigration control functions; and the placement of immigration officials in overseas ports to improve the detection of inadequately documented passengers – all these measures apply indiscriminately to people fleeing persecution and those who seek to travel for other reasons.

4.7　The 1999 Act extended carriers' sanctions to coaches and other road passenger vehicles, and also introduced a new offence of facilitating 'clandestine' entry into the UK.

4.8　*Asylum seeker support provisions.* The 'voucher and dispersal' package established in the 1999 Act constituted a radically new approach to supporting asylum seekers during the application process. First, cash payments through the benefit system were replaced by vouchers (and a small amount of cash). The vouchers could be used only in certain shops, and for which asylum seekers did not receive change. The value of the voucher-plus-cash payment was about 70 per cent of basic income support.

4.9　Second, asylum seekers were required to accept accommodation outside London and south-east England. Even if the accommodation was in an area that lacked essential support services, such as experienced immigration lawyers, rejection by the asylum seeker would mean withdrawal of an offer of accommodation altogether. The newly-establish National Asylum Support Service was not obliged to ensure the availability of key services in the areas to which asylum seekers were sent. Local authorities have made few attempts to inform local residents of the new arrivals and this appears to have caused or exacerbated hostility. Following the murder of an asylum seeker in Glasgow in August 2001, and attacks on asylum seekers in other areas, the government announced that the dispersal system would be reviewed.

4.10   The white paper's justification for the new support system provided a telling insight into the government's overriding concern on asylum. The Home Office acknowledged that the new system would be more cumbersome, and probably more expensive, to administer than traditional cash-based support but argued that it was nevertheless desirable because it would be 'less attractive' for asylum applicants. Amnesty International believes that this emphasis on deterrence is a symptom of the analysis that has driven UK asylum policy in the first term of the Labour administration – an analysis that regards asylum seekers primarily as a 'problem' to be solved, rather than as people whom the UK is legally and morally obliged to respect and protect.

Asylum determination procedures

4.11   Amnesty International believes that one of the major failings of UK asylum policy during the Conservative administration was the deterioration in the quality of the procedures for determining applications. Specific points of concern included the increasingly tight timescales within which applicants were required to present their case; the inadequate use by the Home Office of documented evidence of human rights violations; and the general administration of the process. It was therefore disappointing that the *Fairer, Faster and Firmer* white paper did not include a coherent set of proposals for restoring credibility to the asylum determination system. Instead, there was a commitment to speed up the decision-making process – but with no apparent appreciation that the quality of decisions might suffer as a result.

The 'asylum process pilots'

4.12   This failure to address the integrity of the decision-making process was to become an enduring characteristic of UK asylum practice during Labour's first term. In mid-1999 the Home Office Immigration and Nationality Department (IND) launched a series of what it called 'asylum process pilots'. The stated aims of the pilots included testing different ways of streamlining the determination process; one way was to identify so-called 'straightforward' cases, and making decisions on those quickly – often in just a few days.

4.13   Amnesty International has grave reservations about these fast-track procedures. For example, the practice of interviewing asylum seekers within a day or two of arrival. It is neither fair nor feasible to expect asylum seekers – many of them traumatised – to make a full representation of all relevant aspects of their case in these circumstances. The rationale applied to select applications for streamlined determination gives additional grounds for concern. To a large extent, cases are fast-tracked because the IND considers that they are likely to be 'unfounded'. But this, of course, raises the question: 'how can you tell if a claim is likely to be unfounded before you have even considered it?'. The reply is to be found in the IND's explanatory notes on the pilots: 'nationality will be used as a guide to target cases'.

4.14   To those who recall the last Conservative government's asylum regime, this explanation has a familiar ring. One of the most controversial elements of that regime was the notorious 'White List' – a list of countries whose human rights records were allegedly so unproblematic that asylum applications from their nationals were pre-judged as likely to be without foundation. This assessment was used to justify withdrawing vital appeal rights from those nationals. Labour, then in opposition, was forthright in denouncing the White List, and, technically at least, lived up to its commitment to abolish the list. ('Technically' because the government simultaneously introduced powers for the home secretary similarly to curtail the appeal rights of many applicants.) It is therefore particularly disappointing to see the 'White List principle' restored as a core feature of the asylum determination process.

4.15   The motivation for introducing the asylum process pilots was largely the need to address what was becoming a major political embarrassment for the government – the massive backlog of applications awaiting an initial decision. The backlog of 52,110 (as at 31 May 1998) was described in the white paper as lying at the heart of the problem with the existing immigration and asylum process. And yet, by January 2000, this figure had virtually doubled to 103,495.

4.16   Such a state of affairs would merit urgent attention under any circumstances. In this instance, however, there was a crucial additional factor. The Conservative opposition was increasingly citing the backlog as evidence that the UK had become a 'soft touch' under Labour; and it had made clear an intention to focus on asylum in the run-up to the next general election. The Home Office had to act swiftly.

'Non-compliance' refusals of asylum applications

4.17   A welcome aspect of the Home Office's attempts to reduce the backlog has been the recruitment of substantial numbers of additional asylum caseworkers by the IND. And the 'administrative amnesty' announced in the white paper has also significantly reduced the number of outstanding claims. However, some reduction measures have come at an extremely heavy price in terms of the integrity of the decision-making process.

4.18   Some of the asylum process pilots have introduced a new form which asylum seekers are required to complete as part of the application procedure. The Statement of Evidence Form (SEF) contains a series of questions about the basis of the applicant's claim. In itself, the introduction of the SEF was relatively uncontroversial – indeed, many asylum practitioners saw the procedure as a welcome step towards a more informed approach to decision-making. But in practice it was to prove desperately problematic for asylum seekers and their legal representatives.

4.19   Asylum seekers are required to complete and submit their SEF within just 10 working days – a period during which many asylum seekers will be dispersed from London or south-east England to other parts of the UK. The form, versions of which run to 19 or more pages, must be completed in English, irrespective of the applicant's familiarity with the language. All supporting documentation must be translated into English. Failure to comply with these requirements means that the asylum application is rejected on what are termed 'non-compliance' grounds, without consideration of the merits of the claim. And in all but the most exceptional circumstances, there is no scope for extending the deadlines on grounds such as unavailability of interpreters, lack of access to solicitors, or anything else.

4.20   It is important to stress that non-compliance is an established reason for refusing an asylum claim. As long as there are procedures for pursuing a claim, there will be the potential for applicants to fail to comply with those procedures. The scandal of SEF non-compliance has been the scale of refusals that have resulted. In 1999, there were 1,085 non-compliance refusals. In 2000, the figure was 26,630 – more than 20 times as many. The Home Office does not keep detailed statistics on the reasons for non-compliance refusals, but asylum practitioners report that the great majority have been due to the failure to meet the requirements for completing the SEF.

4.21   The Home Office itself has acknowledged that substantial numbers of SEF non-compliance refusals were wrong: the asylum seeker had, in fact, complied with the requirements but the administrative inadequacies of the IND resulted in a non-compliance refusal being issued.

4.22   The refusal of applications on procedural grounds has had two significant consequences. First, many asylum seekers with well-founded claims will have had their applications rejected. The UK will therefore have failed to live up to its legal obligation under the UN Refugee Convention to grant refuge to people at risk of human rights violations. Second, a substantial proportion will appeal – which means continuing uncertainty for the applicant, and an increased burden on the British taxpayer who foots the bill for running the Immigration Appellate Authority and providing the legal services necessitated by the appeals process. In other words, the massive level of non-compliance refusals runs counter to two basic public policy objectives: it increases the cost of the asylum determination system, and denies protection to those at risk of persecution.

4.23   The level of non-compliance refusals did help to achieve a third policy objective: the political imperative to tackle the 'asylum backlog'. At the beginning of January 2000 the backlog stood at over 100,000; by the end of June 2001 (the month of the general election) the figure was down to 24,315. Of the applications dealt with during these 18 months, a total of 41,135 had been rejected on non-compliance grounds – accounting for more than half of the reduction.

Access to legal advice

4.24   Another element of government policy which Amnesty International criticises is the inadequate provision of access to legal advice for asylum seekers. The *Fairer, Faster and Firmer* white paper stated that 'the Government has considered whether in an asylum system geared to produce swift and fair decisions there is a need to make provision in all cases for legal representatives to be present at asylum interviews. It has concluded that legal representation at the asylum interview is not necessary to enable an applicant to set out his or her case truthfully'.

4.25   The conclusion is flawed. Asylum seekers need legal advice because the asylum determination process is complex and the outcome of an application is determined on the basis of 50 years of international case law interpreting the UN Refugee Convention. Early

access to legal advice would also make the procedure more efficient. Experienced asylum practitioners (including many within the Home Office) agree that the key to an efficient asylum process is to ensure good quality initial decisions – and this in turn means enabling asylum seekers to make a full and coherent statement of their claim at the earliest practical opportunity. Access to legal advice is essential for this.

4.26   An independent review of determination procedures, with a firm focus on administrative efficiency, commissioned by the Home Office also came out in favour of early access to legal advice.[1]

4.27   The dispersal policy has made it more difficult for asylum seekers to obtain good legal advice. By the end of February 2001, 21,410 asylum seekers had been allocated accommodation by the National Asylum Support Service. Most had been sent to areas with no experience of providing support services to asylum seekers. The uncoordinated nature of the dispersal programme has had predictable consequences in terms of the provision of all necessary services, and legal advice has been no exception.

4.28   The few existing practitioners have been overwhelmed by the demand for their services, with the result that asylum seekers in need of legal assistance are routinely turned away. For example, by February 2001 more than 4,000 asylum seekers had been dispersed to the north-east of England. The region had only 13 legal practices with Legal Services Commission contracts to provide legal advice on asylum and immigration and several of those were relatively new to asylum work. One of the few long-established practitioners commented to Amnesty International that they had been unable to take on any new cases for the previous six months. As a result, every week they were turning away about 20 asylum seekers who needed help.

4.29   *Safe in Scotland?*, a report prepared for the Scottish Parliamentary Cross-Party Group on Refugees and Asylum, found that asylum seekers with a legal adviser in England had difficulty communicating by telephone owing to the small amount of cash available to them under the voucher system. Communication by letter was also difficult owing to the lack of translation facilities. Asylum seekers who decided to change their solicitor so they could consult someone locally had to re-apply for legal aid from the Scottish Legal Aid Board. It is feared that as a consequence of these barriers, many asylum seekers in Glasgow have had their claims for asylum refused on the grounds on non-compliance.

4.30   Amnesty International recognises that the Legal Services Commission – the body responsible for promoting the development of community legal services – has taken important steps to extend the provision of legal services to asylum seekers. But it will take time to develop quality legal provision in this complicated and relatively non-lucrative area of the law. For the foreseeable future, the current level of dispersal of asylum seekers will continue to create huge surpluses of demand over supply, with detrimental consequences for asylum seekers and for the effective functioning of the determination system.

Appeals on human rights grounds

4.31   On 2 October 2000, new appeals provisions of the Immigration and Asylum Act 1999 and the Human Rights Act 1998 came into force. Under the new system, an asylum seeker was henceforth entitled to argue that their appeal should be allowed on European Convention on Human Rights grounds as well as or instead of on asylum grounds.

4.32   This marked a significant development in the protection of those fleeing persecution since it meant that the immigration courts could consider and allow appeals on broader human rights criteria and not merely on the restrictive definition of a refugee.

4.33   However, by a commencement order passed shortly before the new provisions came into force, the courts were prevented from considering human rights grounds in the large number of asylum appeals that were pending at the time. The commencement order was challenged in the Immigration Appeals Tribunal and was upheld largely on the basis of a government assurance that appellants would be given the opportunity to make human rights claims if their asylum appeals were dismissed.

4.34   Lawyers acting for asylum applicants subsequently complained of cases where no such opportunity was given and claim that in some cases appellants with outstanding human rights claims or appeals have been unlawfully removed.

4.35   In July 2001, facing a legal challenge, the Home Office conceded that it would not seek to prevent people who had appeals pending on 2 October from from pursuing separate human rights appeals, even where all material factual issues put by the asylum seeker had been rejected in the asylum appeal. However, the concession does not apply to people whose cases had been determined prior to 2 October but where no appeals were pending, although many of them may have strong claims to remain in the UK on human rights grounds.

Racial discrimination

4.36   The Race Relations (Amendment) Act 2000 prohibited racial discrimination by public bodies but exempted decision-making on matters relating to immigration, nationality and asylum. Under a ministerial order, Race Relations (Immigration and Asylum) (No. 2) Authorisation 2000, which came into operation in April 2001, officials carrying out immigration and nationality functions are permitted to discriminate on the basis of nationality or ethnic or national origin. Accordingly, immigration officials lawfully use a list of ethnic groups who may be subjected 'to a more rigorous examination than other persons in the same circumstances'. Among the groups on the list are Roma.

4.37   In February this year the Czech and UK governments concluded an agreement to allow immigration officers attached to the British Embassy to examine passengers intending to fly from Prague to the UK. The pre-clearance was introduced on 18 July after some 640 Czech nationals, all believed to be Roma, applied for asylum in the UK in the first six months of 2001.

4.38   The Home Office assured Amnesty International that the UK immigration control at Prague airport would not operate in a racially discriminatory manner. But information received by the organisation suggests that the majority of people who have been refused leave to enter the UK are Roma. Soon after British immigration officers were placed at Prague airport, two Czech journalists, one from the Roma community, attempted to travel to the UK. The Romani journalist was barred. Both carried hidden cameras and the incident was shown on Czech TV. It was generally regarded as evidence that Roma are targeted and aroused considerable controversy. The pre-clearance scheme was suspended on 9 August but according to reports at the time of writing has been reinstated.

4.39   The Home Office confirmed to Amnesty International that individual passengers who indicated that they intended to seek asylum would not normally be allowed to board flights to the UK. Therefore, among those denied access to the UK are Roma who may be fleeing human rights violations and entitled to international protection under the 1951 UN Convention on Refugees or who would qualify for protection under other international human rights treaties

4.40   In May 2001, the Court of Appeal allowed the asylum claim of a Czech Roma who,

along with his family, had been subjected to racist attacks and discrimination for years, including assault by the police, who were supposed to protect him. Indeed, just two days after the screening by British immigration officials began, Ota Absolon, a 30 year old Romani man, was stabbed to death in an apparently racially-motivated attack in East Bohemia. The person charged with the killing had earlier been given a suspended sentence for stabbing another Romani man in the stomach. At the end of July 2001, the UN Human Rights Committee noted it was 'deeply concerned about discrimination against minorities, particularly Roma…and about the persistent allegations of police harassment, particularly of the Roma minority…'.

Detention of asylum seekers

4.41   While the majority of people seeking asylum in the UK are admitted temporarily pending determination of their application, a significant and increasing number are detained.

4.42   When the government was elected in 1997, between 750 and 850 asylum seekers were detained in the UK at any time. At the end of May 2001, the number was approximately 1,200. The numbers are estimated because the data provided by the government does not distinguish between asylum seekers and others detained under the Immigration Act powers.

4.43   The 'detention estate' – the number of places allocated for people detained under the Immigration Act – is due to increase to 2,790 by the end of the year and on current trends some 2,000 of them will be asylum applicants.

4.44   Amnesty International has three major concerns about the detention of asylum seekers: whether detention is used appropriately; the length of detention; and detention in prison.

Appropriateness of detention

4.45   International standards permit detention only in certain circumstances. According to the Executive Committee for the office of the UN High Commissioner for Refugees (UNHCR), 'in view of the hardship which it involves, detention should normally be avoided. If necessary, detention should be resorted to only on grounds prescribed by law to verify identity; to determine the elements on which the claim to refugee status or asylum is based; to deal with cases where refugees or asylum seekers have destroyed their travel documents in order to mislead the authorities of the State in which they intend to claim asylum; or to protect national security or public order.'

4.46   In 1997, Amnesty International's research showed that in many cases, detention was arbitrary, prolonged, costly and ultimately futile; that the majority had been detained before the merits of their claim had been assessed and that amongst those asylum seekers held in detention were individuals later recognised as refugees in the UK.[2]

4.47   The white paper *Fairer, Faster and Firmer* indicated that the government was mindful of these concerns, stating that 'the deprivation of liberty is a grave step which must only be used with great care and when no alternative ways of ensuring compliance are likely to be effective.' Subsequently, the government stated that the increase in the detention of asylum seekers was necessary to facilitate the removal of refused applicants and that the focus of detention was therefore at the end of the process.

4.48   However, government policy and practice suggest that detention continues to be used inappropriately, in violation of international standards. Although comprehensive statistics are not available, the data that has been released shows that the majority of asylum seekers are detained in the initial stages of the process. That was so in February 1998 (51 per cent were awaiting an initial decision on their application), January 1999 (57 per cent) and March 1999 (60 per cent).

4.49   In 2000, Leanne Weber and Loraine Gelsthorpe of Cambridge University interviewed 25 chief immigration officers and 35 immigration officers at a number of ports of entry about the main purposes of detention.[3] Fifteen per cent stated that encouraging someone to withdraw their application for asylum was a main purpose and a further 13 per cent gave deterring other people from seeking asylum as a main purpose. Both these purposes are unlawful.

4.50   Oakington Detention Centre opened in March 2000. In March 2001, the then home office minister, Barbara Roche, said that applicants were referred to Oakington where it appeared that their application could be 'decided quickly, including those which may be certified as manifestly unfounded'. Over 7,000 people have been held at Oakington.

4.51   In 2001 four Iraqi Kurds challenged the legality of their detention at Oakington under the Human Rights Act. In September 2001, Mr Justice Collins of the high court decided that their detention violated their rights as protected by the European Convention on Human Rights.

Under the convention, detention is justified if a person might otherwise effect an unlawful entry or because action is being taken to remove them. However, the Iraqis were detained to enable a speedy determination of their applications and this was an unlawful purpose. The Home Office has lodged an appeal against the decision. Amnesty International notes that all four Iraqis were refused asylum and then appealed. Three of the four Iraqis have now had their appeals against their initial refusal of asylum allowed and the final appeal is still outstanding.

4.52   The Immigration and Asylum Act provided for two automatic bail hearings before a court and a right to bail without sureties except in certain defined cases. This was to come into force in April 2001 but was deferred initially to October 2001, owing to the expansion of the detention estate. There is still no date for implementation. Pending the introduction of automatic bail hearings detainees may apply for bail under the Immigration Act 1971. The immigration service does not assist detainees to apply and in practice, only detainees who secure legal representation have access to bail procedures.

Length of detention

4.53   In December 1998, following a visit to the UK, the United Nations Working Group on Arbitrary Detention stated its concern that '[t]he functioning of the legal regime on occasion makes the restriction on liberty and free movement sufficiently prolonged that it might in specific instances result in arbitrary deprivation of liberty'.[4]

4.54   Statistics are not available to assess whether the average length of detention has changed but in July 2000 the UNHCR noted that 'the UK detains more people for longer periods and with less judicial supervision than any comparable country in Europe'. The UNHCR indicated that at September 1999 asylum seekers were detained for an average of 65 days with more than 275-325 asylum seekers spending more than three months in detention. Ten had been detained for more than a year.

Detention in prison

4.55   According to the executive committee of the UNHCR, 'refugees and asylum seekers shall, whenever possible, not be accommodated with persons detained as common criminals and shall not be located in areas where their physical safety is endangered'.[5]

4.56   When the government came into office approximately 300 of the asylum seekers detained at any time were held in prisons, although their only 'crime' was to have sought asylum in the UK. In 1998 the government stated that it accepted a recommendation of the chief inspector of prisons, Sir David Ramsbotham, that the number of asylum seekers held in prisons should be considerably reduced. In 1999, during the passage of the Immigration and Asylum Bill, Lord Williams of Mostyn told parliament that the government had accepted the principle that no detainee ought to be kept in the prison regime. 'That cannot be brought about overnight', he stated, 'but we accepted the principle immediately and there was not the slightest demur. David Ramsbotham was absolutely right and we said so at the time.' However, the number grew. In November 2000, 500 extra prison places were phased in for immigration detainees in a number of prisons around the country including Belmarsh, Winchester and Cardiff. The use of these places for immigration detainees are due to end in October 2001 when the new immigration service detention centres at Harmonsdsworth, Yarl's Wood, Dungavel and Aldington are due to come on stream. Ramsbotham reiterated his opposition in 2001: 'I don't believe it's right to hold people who have not been accused of or committed a crime in prison conditions.'[6]

4.57   In July 2001, the parliamentary under-secretary for the Home Department, Angela Eagle, said that she hoped that 'by Christmas' no asylum seekers would be detained in Cardiff prison, which had been the subject of media attention when asylum seekers were handcuffed when they were taken to a local hospital. She said she was not able to give the same commitment for other prisons.

Libyan asylum applicants

4.58   In April 2000 Amnesty International wrote to the Home Office regarding concerns about returning asylum seekers to Libya following the removal of a Libyan applicant who, the organisation believed, would be at risk of serious human rights violations. Amnesty International believes he was detained on arrival in Libya. A year later, the Home Office informed Amnesty International that rejected Libyan asylum seekers would not be returned to Libya and would be granted six months exceptional leave to remain in the UK while the government monitors the situation over the next 12 months.

4.59   The Home Office stated that the Foreign and Commonwealth Office had advised that Libyans returning to that country after an absence of six months or more are subject to interrogation by the Libyan security authorities. Failed asylum seekers are routinely imprisoned by administrative (as opposed to judicial) order

for 'having shown disloyalty to the state'. The FCO said that it does not expect a significant change in the human rights situation in Libya within the next 12 months. On this basis Amnesty International believes that Libyan applicants could claim that they qualify not for exceptional leave, but for refugee status under the 1951 convention.

European and international developments

'...I regret to say there are some indications that Europe is losing sight of its duty to protect refugees under international law as set out in the 1951 Convention on Refugees. This is a source of deep concern to me and risks having enormous impact on other regions who look to Europe as an example.'
– *UN secretary-general Kofi Annan at the Stockholm International Forum on Combating Intolerance, 2001.*

4.60   In 1997 EU member states agreed the Amsterdam Treaty, which brought asylum within the competence of the European Commission, the European parliament and the Council of Ministers. The treaty, which came into force in May 1999, requires members to adopt a number of legally binding measures on asylum and refugee protection within five years. These include minimum standards on procedures for granting and withdrawing refugee status, the definition of a refugee, and reception conditions.

4.61   At Tampere in October 1999, EU member states agreed to work towards the establishment by a two stage process of a common European asylum system. In the short term this would include minimum standards to be adopted by member states leading to a common asylum procedure and a uniform status for those granted asylum, valid throughout the EU.

4.62   At the Tampere summit, EU governments reaffirmed the importance that EU member states attach to the absolute respect of the right to seek asylum. They agreed to work towards an asylum system based on the comprehensive application of the 1951 UN Convention on Refugees, thus ensuring that nobody would be returned to a country where they might be persecuted. Amnesty International welcomed this commitment but the initial steps towards harmonisation have failed to ensure that it will be comprehensively implemented. The organisation is concerned that the harmonisation of asylum policies at EU level may result in the lowest common denominator rather than adequate protection for refugees.

4.63 In September 2000 the European Commission issued a draft directive on minimum standards on procedures for granting and withdrawing refugee status. Amnesty International reviewed the directive and identified some proposed provisions that fall short of international refugee and human rights law. For example, the proposals would not provide effective access to a fair procedure as some asylum seekers would be subjected to admissibility criteria and do not ensure that all asylum seekers would be allowed to stay in the EU until the outcome of their appeal.

4.64 Earlier this year the House of Lords select committee on the EU conducted an inquiry into the proposed minimum standards on asylum procedures. It took evidence from, among others, the president of the Immigration Appeal Tribunal; Barbara Roche, then minister of state at the Home Office; and Amnesty International. The committee's report, published in March, endorsed many of the concerns of Amnesty International and other organisations stating, 'There is much to welcome in the draft Directive's definition of basic principles and procedural guarantees. But there are also risks in the latitude given to Member States to derogate from important safeguards.' The committee stressed that the concept of 'minimum standards' should not be defined in terms of the lowest common denominator but that the directive should endeavour to raise standards.

4.65 The first package of legally binding EU asylum and immigration measures was agreed by EU ministers in May 2001. On 20 July the directive on minimum standards for temporary protection in the event of a mass influx of displaced persons was adopted. Amnesty International had expressed its concern at governments' increasing tendency to abandon the internationally recognised regime for the protection of refugees and their propensity to resort to alternative protection regimes, such as temporary protection, which are not ruled by international law. Amnesty International believes that the minimum standards in the field of asylum must be at least those currently provided by international law.

4.66 The year 2001 is the 50th anniversary of the 1951 UN Convention on Refugees and the UNHCR launched a global consultation on international protection. The primary goal of the exercise is to renew and revitalise the international regime for the protection of refugees. The consultations are being conducted along three tracks. The first seeks to strengthen the commitment of states to respect the centrality of the 1951 convention and its 1967 protocol in the international refugee protection system.

4.67 Despite commitments by states to the observance of international refugee and human rights law many states, including the UK, have introduced obstacles to refugees seeking protection on their territory. The obstacles include:
• visa regimes;
• carrier sanctions which fail to discriminate between those fleeing human rights violations and others, often forcing those in need of protection into the hands of illegal traffickers;
• safe country of origin and safe third country concepts;
• accelerated asylum procedures which do not fulfil the minimum requirements of a fair and satisfactory asylum procedure;
• the increased use of lesser forms of protection which are not ruled by international law.

4.68 During 2000-2001 the then home secretary, Jack Straw, said that the 1951 convention was out of date and that he would urge ministers from other countries to revise it. His proposals for a more rational and effective protection regime identified three areas in which the international community should do better:
• help the countries concerned to make conditions in the regions of origin better;
• make it easier for genuine refugees to access the protection regimes of European and other western states, for example by making their journey less hazardous;
• ensure that those who are not refugees are actively dissuaded from seeking to benefit unjustly from the terms of the 1951 convention.

4.69 An element of Mr Straw's second point – improving refugees' access to western protection – refers to a proposed resettlement programme for the EU. In October 2000, the Home Office issued a discussion paper outlining a resettlement programme for people from high-risk countries and groups to the EU. Applicants from countries categorised as safe would be inadmissible. The following month the European Commission's paper on a common asylum system for the EU referred to a possible resettlement programme and stated that it would conduct feasibility studies.

4.70 Eighteen countries world-wide operate proactive refugee programmes based on bilateral quota arrangements with the UNHCR. The Home Office paper mentions that Australia and the USA accept refugees under humanitarian programmes, as well as accepting spontaneous applicants. In its response to the document, Amnesty International supported the concept of a resettlement programme for refugees but on the basis for people identified to be in need of international protection, not on the categorisation of countries and groups of origin.

Amnesty International was also concerned that a resettlement programme should not prejudice asylum seekers who arrive spontaneously in the EU and that such a programme should not be established solely to deter unselected arrivals rather than to enhance protection. In Australia for example, spontaneous asylum seekers are detained until determination of their claim. Amnesty International views a resettlement programme as an addition to and not a replacement for a properly resourced, fair and satisfactory asylum procedure to examine on their merits asylum applications from those who seek protection in the EU.

4.71   On 12 December 2001, the UNHCR and the Swiss government will convene the first formal meeting of the more than 140 states that have acceded to the UN Convention on Refugees and its 1967 protocol. The meeting will commemorate the 50th anniversary of the convention and the signatories will issue a declaration reaffirming their commitment to the full and effective implementation of its values.

4.72   The UK government should take this opportunity not only to commit itself to implementation of the convention, but also to call upon states to join it in putting more effort into preventing the causes of refugee movements than in deterring refugees.

4.73   In December also, EU heads of state will meet in Laeken, Belgium, to assess the implementation of the asylum provisions in the Amsterdam Treaty, as a follow-up to the decisions reached in Tampere in October 1999. The UK government should take a leading role in advocating that EU member states should translate their expressed commitment to international refugee and human rights obligations into specific standards that ensure maximum protection for refugees. As the House of Lords select committee on the EU stated in its report on minimum standards in asylum procedures: 'It is in the interests of all Member States as well as refugees that any Community regime seeks to promote the highest possible standards not the lowest common denominator…'. Further, the UK should advocate that any resettlement programme for the EU should not be to the detriment of asylum seekers arriving spontaneously.

Prospects for the second term

4.74   There can be little doubt that asylum policy will retain its place in the political spotlight during the second term of the Labour administration. Human rights violations around the world will continue to force millions of people to flee their homes in search of protection. And although it will remain the case that only a small proportion of the displaced seek refuge in western Europe, many politicians and members of the public will consider the numbers to be unacceptably high, and will regard the asylum seekers themselves as 'bogus', 'abusive' or 'illegal'. At the same time, racial tensions in the UK are likely to increase.

4.75   In other words, key elements of the political environment in which asylum policy is formulated are likely to remain unchanged. The imposition of the extraordinary 'pre-entry' immigration controls on Czech Republic nationals, described above, is a worrying indication. A key pledge in the 2001 manifesto was that substantially larger numbers of rejected asylum seekers would be removed from Britain. In view of the short-comings of the UK's determination procedures, pursuit of this objective is likely to mean that people in need of protection will be returned to face the risk of human rights violations.

The policy context

4.76   Some developments, however, suggest that there may be an opportunity, at least, to press for a more balanced approach to asylum policy, one that would attach as much weight to the UK's obligations to the victims of human rights violations as it does to deterring those who would seek to 'abuse the system'.

4.77   One such development is that the government is prepared to advocate the benefits of limited immigration on economic grounds. This was signalled by the then home office minister, Barbara Roche, in a speech to the Institute for Public Policy Research in September 2000.

4.78   The implications for asylum policy are not straightforward. It is one thing to recognise that it is in the national interest to allow prescribed numbers of economic migrants to come to the UK to do the jobs that British citizens do not want to do, or to contribute skills which are currently in short supply domestically. It is quite another thing to promote the UK's obligations towards refugees in the face of widespread public hostility.

4.79   Nevertheless, the move towards a more open approach to immigration is an important first step in cultivating a more informed, less prejudiced, public debate on immigration. The crucial second step is to live up to this responsibility – through specific measures to address widespread public misconceptions about refugees; and by implementing asylum practices that are consistent with government statements about upholding the UN Convention on Refugees and valuing the contribution that refugees make to UK society.

Racism and asylum

4.80   During the past year or so, domestic and international observers have expressed concern that hardline political rhetoric and public policy on asylum have fuelled racial tension, including racial violence, around the UK. Such comments have come from the UN Committee for the Elimination of Racial Discrimination and the European Commission against Racism and Intolerance, among others. In the view of officers of the Metropolitan Police Racial and Violent Crimes Unit: 'The most serious trend we have seen is a rise in reports of incidents when the issue of asylum-seekers and refugees is brought into the public domain by reputable politicians making inflammatory statements.'

4.81   This analysis must be taken into account by those responsible for formulating UK asylum policy. If a link is recognised between an asylum policy that treats and portrays asylum seekers as a 'problem', and increased racial violence, a government which is concerned about rising racial tension needs to adopt a less hostile approach towards asylum seekers.

A more collaborative approach to asylum policy

4.82   Ostensibly, an encouraging aspect of the Labour administration's attitude to asylum policy has been its promotion of a more collaborative relationship with agencies that seek to represent the interests of refugees and asylum seekers. The publication of the 1998 white paper followed a period of consultation with refugee agencies and communities. The government subsequently agreed to include an atypical 'special standing committee' phase in the parliamentary schedule of the 1999 Immigration and Asylum Bill – giving non-governmental organisations an opportunity to inform the forthcoming consideration of the bill. And the IND has established several consultative groups, bringing together the officials responsible for implementing (and helping to formulate) policy, and the 'external'

agencies that can feed the day-to-day experiences of asylum seekers into that process.

4.83   Regrettably, the perception of the non-governmental agencies that have participated in these initiatives is that they have failed to live up to their stated intentions. Given the considerable time and energy invested by all concerned, there is scant evidence that either the formulation or the implementation of asylum policy has taken account of the perspective provided by the 'refugee sector' in any meaningful way.

4.84   This must be rectified. A recent development may prove to be crucial. For the first time, the Home Office has established an extensive programme of research into the basis for, and the effects of, UK asylum policy. This is welcome in itself, but all the more so because of the emphasis placed on constructive collaboration between all interested parties.

The way forward

4.85   At the time of writing, it is too early to assess how asylum policy and practice will develop in response to the many factors affecting the decision-makers and those who influence them. Reviews of the dispersal programme and the voucher system, among others, are not yet complete.

4.86   It is essential that the government makes an explicit public commitment to examine all aspects of asylum policy and practice in order to ensure that they are consistent with the UK's obligations towards the victims of human rights abuses. To that end, Amnesty International proposes five principles for refugee protection as the basis of a fair, efficient and humane asylum system:
• Every asylum application should be considered fully on its individual merits, and not pre-judged on the basis of nationality.
• All asylum seekers should have access to legal advice.
• Asylum seekers should not be detained without just cause.
• Immigration controls should not prevent asylum seekers from escaping persecution.
• The 1951 Refugee Convention should be upheld, and properly implemented.

Recommendations

Statement of Evidence forms

■ The standard period within which an asylum seeker must complete a Statement of Evidence Form should be extended.

■ An asylum seeker should be entitled to an extension of time to complete a form if she or he can demonstrate special circumstances.

Access to legal advice

■ Asylum seekers should not be required to live in areas where they cannot have ready access to expert legal advice relating to their claims.

Racial discrimination

■ The Race Relations Act should be amended to prohibit public officials from discriminating on the grounds of race in the exercise of their functions on matters relating to immigration and asylum.

Detention

■ In view of the hardship it involves, detention should be avoided. No asylum seeker should be detained unless it has been established that detention is lawful and complies with international standards.

■ The government should implement the law providing for automatic bail hearings as soon as possible.

■ Asylum seekers should not be detained in prisons with people convicted of criminal offences.

European and international standards

■ At the meeting of states parties to the Refugee Convention in December 2001, the UK should reaffirm its commitment to the full and effective implementation of the convention and call upon states to join it in putting greater effort into preventing the causes of refugee movements.

■ At the European Union heads of state meeting in December 2001 the UK government should take a leading role in advocating that EU member states translate their expressed commitment to international refugee and human rights obligations into specific standards that ensure maximum protection for refugees.

■ The UK government should advocate that any resettlement programme for the EU should not be to the detriment of asylum seekers arriving spontaneously.

5 Business and human rights

Controlling the arms trade

5.1   The *Amnesty International Report 2001* documents human rights violations, including torture and killings, in 149 countries and territories. Military, security and police forces often use foreign arms and skills learned from foreigners to commit these violations. Some governments and companies recruit foreign mercenaries who may operate almost with impunity.

5.2   The effective control of international movements of arms, training and personnel is therefore a vital element of efforts to stop human rights violations. The UK is one of the world's top arms exporting nations, so its government has a particular responsibility to regulate the transfer of weapons technology and training from this country in order to ensure that British weapons and expertise do not contribute to human rights violations abroad. It also has a responsibility to work for the development of effective regulatory systems by regional and international intergovernmental institutions.

5.3   The risk of UK-supplied equipment being used for human rights violations is real. In Indonesia in 1996-97, UK-supplied Tactica water cannon and armoured vehicles were used to suppress demonstrations, resulting in the deaths of several protestors and injuries to scores of others. More recently, in July 1999, the chief of the Indonesian armed forces confirmed that UK-supplied Hawk jets had been used in East Timor in violation of end-use assurances given by the Indonesian government. In Kenya, the use of UK-supplied tear gas against civilian demonstrators has been a matter of concern to Amnesty International.

5.4   Despite these events, the UK has continued to export these types of equipment, spare parts and accessories to Indonesia and Kenya. In 1999, the UK exported 10 Hawk jets to Indonesia under a deal licensed by the previous Conservative administration. In 2000, licences were granted for the export of combat aircraft components to Indonesia and stun grenades to Kenya.

5.5   When Labour came to power, arms exports were governed by legislation that had been in place since the Second World War – the Import, Export and Customs (Powers) Defence Act 1939. The legislation was seriously deficient with respect to brokering – people in the UK arranging sales of equipment from one country to another, without that equipment passing through the UK – and licensed production – UK companies providing companies in other countries with the expertise, technology and production equipment to manufacture arms under licence. Also, there was no effective monitoring of the ultimate destination of exported weapons and the use made of them.

5.6   Deficiencies in export control were identified in 1996 by the Scott inquiry into the so-called arms-to-Iraq scandal. The Scott report recommended major changes which the Labour party strongly supported while in opposition. In power, Labour has been slow to reform controls on arms exports. The only exception was the prohibition on export of certain equipment that had been used for torture, such as electro-shock devices.

5.7   The government released a white paper proposing new export controls in July 1998. Legislation – the Export Control and Non-proliferation Bill – was introduced into parliament only in June 2001, after Labour's election to a second term of office. The bill gives the secretary of state new powers to impose export controls. The details of these controls will be contained in secondary legislation that remains unpublished at the time of writing. It is impossible to judge the impact of the bill without seeing how the secondary legislation will flesh out the powers granted under the primary legislation.

5.8   This chapter looks at the following issues:
• the export and brokering of equipment which is commonly used to inflict torture;
• the export, brokering and licensing of the manufacture of equipment that has legitimate uses but may be abused to commit human rights violations;
• the UK and the international prohibition of anti-personnel landmines;
• the UK and international efforts to restrict the

trade in small arms;
• controlling the activities of mercenaries.

Equipment for torture and ill-treatment

5.9   The devices used by torturers range from the very simple – shackles, thumbscrews and whips – to sophisticated electro-shock equipment. The use of chains and irons as restraints is prohibited under the internationally agreed Standard Minimum Rules for the Treatment of Prisoners. Recent Amnesty International research found that the number of companies world-wide known to be producing or supplying electro-shock equipment had risen from 30 in the 1980s to more than 130 in 2000. Mechanical restraints such as leg irons are also still widely used.[1]

5.10   During the 1990s, British companies were implicated in the trade in electro-shock weapons and mechanical restraints. In July 1997, then foreign secretary Robin Cook said that the government was 'committed to preventing British companies from manufacturing, selling or procuring equipment designed primarily for torture and to press for a global ban.' He announced that the government would act to prevent the export or transhipment from the UK of certain equipment designed or used for torture or other cruel, inhuman or degrading treatment or punishment. The equipment included various electro-shock devices such as stun guns and tasers (dart-firing stun guns), as well as leg-irons and shackles.

5.11   However, the ban did not apply to dealers in the UK brokering the supply of such equipment, as long as the goods themselves did not touch UK soil. The 1998 White Paper on Strategic Export Controls contained proposals to prohibit the brokering of equipment used for torture, but the delay in bringing a bill before parliament has left brokers and traffickers free to continue their activities.

5.12   In September 2000, The Observer[2] reported that a UK company offered to arrange the delivery of leg-irons and CS gas to a private security company in Rwanda. Amnesty International has documented the use of these items by government security forces and armed political groups in that country to commit serious human rights violations. The sale of this type of equipment to a private security company in Rwanda breaches a UN arms embargo that prohibits the delivery of weapons to anyone other than the Rwandese government or UN peace-keeping forces.

5.13   In October 2000, Amnesty International staff discovered that an exhibitor was marketing 'nickel plated legcuffs' at the International Police and Security Expo 2000. The show was organised in association with a conference of the Association of Chief Police Officers, and a published guide claimed to see the 'continuation and development of close co-operation between the police and leading suppliers'.[3] Speakers at the conference included five chief constables and the then home secretary, Jack Straw. The company's catalogue claimed the legcuffs to be 'Kick proof, pick proof, walk proof and run proof' and to 'fit[s] any size of leg'.[4]

5.14   The government has stated that it will use the powers provided under the Export Control and Non-proliferation Bill to 'introduce controls on trafficking and brokering of equipment whose export the Government ha[s] already banned because of evidence of its use in torture'. Amnesty International welcomes this commitment. It urges the government to impose controls on brokering and trafficking promptly after legislation is passed and to define these practices as explicitly including promotion and marketing.

5.15   In view of the government's stated concerns about electro-shock weapons, it seems anomalous that some UK police forces were recently reported to be considering deploying dart-firing electro-shock stun guns. The harm that tasers may inflict has not been researched independently and Amnesty International has called on the police authorities not to proceed without such an investigation. Amnesty International also urges the government to take into account that if it permits the use of tasers in the UK, this will undermine its credibility to lead international efforts to control the proliferation and use of electro-shock devices.

5.16   In addition to national controls, stringent regional and international controls are required on the flow of equipment designed and used for torture. The UK government has actively supported the adoption of a European-wide ban on the export of equipment used for torture. Amnesty International urges the UK government to continue to press for the EU to implement such a ban as soon as possible.

Arms and security equipment
Export criteria

5.17   In July 1997 Mr Cook announced new guidelines for the assessment of export licence applications for arms and security equipment. The criteria included 'the respect of human rights and fundamental freedoms in the country of final destination' and the guidelines stated that the government would not issue an export licence if there was a 'clear risk that the proposed export might be used for internal repression'. Amnesty International welcomed both the guidelines and their publication, a change from the secretive practices of previous administrations.

5.18   The guidelines still left room for improvement, however. For example, the phrase 'internal repression', which is not used in international human rights or humanitarian law, was ambiguous. It left a loophole in the export control system which would allow the transfer of arms and security equipment that might be used to commit human rights violations.

5.19   The guidelines also permitted the export of equipment to states claiming it was for the protection of their security force personnel, even where there were strong grounds for concern that the equipment might be used for internal repression. Both these loopholes were closed in 2000, when the government adopted revised criteria incorporating the EU Code of Conduct on Arms Exports.

Prior scrutiny

5.20   The harm that may result from the misuse of arms and other security equipment is so great that licence applications should be thoroughly scrutinised and permission to export should be granted only after all pertinent information and points of view have been considered. The appropriate forum for such scrutiny is parliament.

5.21   Prior scrutiny by the legislature occurs in Sweden and the United States. The Quadripartite Select Committee (QSC) – an all-party committee made up of MPs from the committees on defence, foreign affairs, international development and trade and industry – visited Sweden and the USA to study the systems in operation there, and subsequently proposed such a system for the UK on several occasions. The government has consistently rejected the proposals, most recently in July 2001 when it stated that it 'remains convinced that prior parliamentary scrutiny of export licence applications would not be right in principle, and could not be made to work in practice'.[5]

5.22   The Defence Manufacturers' Association has strongly opposed prior parliamentary and public scrutiny, suggesting that it might 'create opportunities for unrepresentative pressure groups unduly to influence policy or decisions. It is important to maintain a pragmatic, realistic and rational approach to defence exports and to avoid being swept along by the idealistic and emotive arguments of a vocal minority'.[6]

5.23   Amnesty International believes that the QSC's proposals would meet the legitimate concerns of the government and the Defence Manufacturers' Association about such issues as inordinate delay and breaches of commercial confidentiality. We urge the government to reconsider its position and introduce a system of prior parliamentary scrutiny in the next parliamentary session.

Annual reports

5.24   Transparency in government policy and practice is essential to hold the government accountable for its conduct. In July 1998 Robin Cook acknowledged that an 'informed public debate is the best guarantee of responsible regulation of the arms trade' and committed the government to publishing an annual report on the application of export controls. The first *Annual Report on Strategic Export Controls* was published in March 1999 and covered export licences granted between May and December 1997. Since then the government has published three reports. The most recent, which appeared on 20 July 2001, covers export licences granted between 1 January and 31 December 2000. The Export Control and Non-proliferation Bill places a legal obligation on the government to publish annual reports.

5.25   The first report was an important step towards creating a transparent export control system but the information was unacceptably dated, some data was aggregated in a manner that obscured key elements and there were significant omissions. Observers could not be sure that UK exports were not being used to commit human rights violations. The three subsequent reports provide better accounts but the data does not yet permit thorough scrutiny.

5.26   The table below, based on the information in the annual reports, shows the number of licences granted and refused between 2 May 1997 and 31 December 2000, for the supply of arms and security equipment to countries where Amnesty International is concerned that they might be used to commit serious human rights violations.

5.27   Like preceding reports, the report for 2000 fails to provide details of the end-users of the equipment licensed for export. The QSC has recommended that this information be included. The equivalent report published in the USA does provide details of end-users.

5.28   End-user details are essential to assess the human rights impact of export licences. For example, the *Amnesty International Report 2001* documents shootings and killings by the Kenyan police that appeared to contravene international

Export licences issued and refused for Military List items since 2 May 1997

Country	Standard Individual Export Licences Military List 2 May 1997-31 December 2000		Open Individual Export Licences Military List 2 May 1997-31 December 1999	
	Licences issued	Licences refused	Licences issued	Licences refused/revoked
Bahrain	92	1	41	0
Colombia	34	6	17	0
India	2181	13	105	2
Indonesia	119	10	30	2
Kenya	109	2	37	0
Pakistan	312	37	45	1
Saudi Arabia	139	0	91	0
Sri Lanka	170	5	16	1
Turkey	401	2	89	2
Totals	3557	76	471	8

human rights standards. The government's report on arms exports for 2000 lists export licences granted for small arms ammunition, shotguns, a semi-automatic pistol and components for rifles and general purpose machine guns to Kenya. Without details of the end-users, it is impossible to tell whether the equipment is destined for game wardens, which would be unlikely to cause concern, or for police units who took part in the human rights violations that Amnesty International reported.

5.29   The government's report for 2000 included certain additional information about equipment licensed for export. However, unlike the previous reports, it omitted the Military and Dual-use List ratings that group the equipment into broad categories which are given alphanumeric codes, for example 'arms and automatic weapons with a calibre of 12.7mm or less' are coded ML1 and 'ground vehicles and components therefor specially designed or modified for military use' are ML6. These codes are important because they facilitate analysis and scrutiny of licensing decisions. When linked to the summary descriptions, they also help to identify the nature of the export licences granted.

5.30   The government stated that the codes were omitted because of the 'increased detail provided on items licensed for export'.[7] The explanation is not persuasive. The substitution of one type of information for another hinders the comparison and analysis of trends in UK export licensing policy from one year to the next. The summary descriptions are neither consistent nor coherent. While some of the descriptions are relatively explicit, such as 'shotguns' and 'anti-g/pressure suits', others are ambiguous, for example 'components for combat helicopter' and 'military communications equipment'.

5.31   There is no apparent reason why the annual report could not contain additional information about the equipment being exported. The Irish government publishes far more detail about goods licensed for export on a monthly basis and even offers to prepare the export licensing statistics in a format of the user's choice.

5.32   Additional information and a more meaningful breakdown of the data in the annual reports would also help to protect the government from unfair criticism for granting

Monitoring arms flows

5.33   The information presented in the annual report makes it difficult to monitor arms flows to a particular destination. For example, the Scott report investigated the possibility that arms and related equipment are transhipped via Austria to undesirable end-users, but it is difficult to work out from the *Strategic Export Controls Annual Report* whether there is cause for concern that British arms are being transferred in this way.

5.34   The report provides information about:
• equipment licensed for export under Standard Individual Export Licences (SIEL), which permit shipment of a specified quantity of items to a specified consignee. The 2000 report lists the number of small arms exported under SIELs.
• the number of Open Individual Export Licenses (OIEL),

which permit an exporter to make multiple shipments of specified items to a specified destination for a particular period. The actual number of weapons shipped is not publicly reported.

5.35   The summary description of goods licensed for export to Austria shown in the annual report for 2000 lists nine SIELs for small arms covering a total of 29 weapons and 59 OIELs granted for shotguns, single shot and semi-automatic firearms and ammunition. From this information, it is impossible to determine the quantity of small arms and ammunition being exported to Austria. It is therefore impossible to tell if the transfers meet the legitimate requirements of the Austrian armed forces or whether there is cause for concern about transhipment.

licences which seem to give cause for concern. The QSC noted that its members' concerns about particular licences granted were often easily assuaged: 'the simple revelation of the quantities concerned or the intended end-user were evidence enough of the reason for the grant of the licence.'[8]

Monitoring use

5.36   The Scott inquiry identified two serious flaws in the monitoring of the use of exported arms. First, technologies that might be used to produce weapons could be exported without adequate scrutiny of the uses to which they would be put. This weakness also applies to exports of arms and security equipment that can be used to commit human rights violations. Second, arms and ammunition could readily be diverted or re-exported from the recipient country.

5.37   Labour's 1997 manifesto committed it to 'strengthen the monitoring of the end-use of defence exports to prevent diversion to third countries and to ensure that exported equipment is used only on the conditions under which the export licence has been granted.' The government believes that the best way to prevent diversion is to strengthen the process of risk assessment at the licence application stage. The 1999 annual report has a section headed 'Minimising the risk of diversion' which states that before granting or refusing a licence, the government now regularly seeks additional details of proposed end-users from its overseas missions. There is no systematic approach to the monitoring of arms and security equipment once it leaves the UK, but the report does list examples of circumstances where the government believed that post-export monitoring

would be useful to inform future licensing decisions. Monitoring methods include visits by UK officials to check on the use of UK-supplied equipment, and regular contacts between customers and UK defence attachés allowing them to confirm that UK-supplied equipment has not been diverted.

5.38   The report for 2000 does not have a section on 'Minimising the risk of diversion', and earlier this year trade secretary Stephen Byers told the QSC that the government was satisfied with the system as it stands. Giving oral evidence on the draft bill he said: 'We have looked very carefully at the whole area of end-user requirements and the view that we have come to ... is that the measures that we already have in place will be sufficient.'[9]

5.39   Amnesty International strongly disagrees. Recent developments in Israel and the Occupied Territories highlight inadequacies in the UK system of end-use monitoring. Amnesty International has expressed concern about the use of lethal force by the Israeli authorities in violation of international law.[10]

5.40   The UK government issued export licences for components for combat helicopters and related technology to Israel in 1999 and 2000. Two Open Individual Export Licences are currently in force for the same equipment. The UK also granted licences for the export of small arms ammunition and components for air-to-surface missiles. Because the annual report lacks detailed information, it is impossible to tell which components have been licensed for export. Faced with persistent questioning by MPs, the government assured parliament that it is

monitoring the situation carefully and has 'no evidence that equipment or components licensed for export to Israel by this Government have been used by Israeli security forces against civilians in the occupied territories or in southern Lebanon'.[11] It has also sought and received assurances from the Israeli authorities that UK-supplied equipment is not being used against civilians. However, in his oral evidence to the QSC Robin Cook admitted that the government has no independent way of verifying this claim:
'On the question of what we can do on the ground, our Defence Attaché is meant to ensure he maintains a close interest in what is occurring in the Occupied Territories, but I have to be candid with the Committee and say, having licensed equipment there is a limit to the extent to which we can then subsequently, when it has left our shores, verify where it is or on what plane or wherever it is flying. We seek to but I cannot pretend to say that I have as good a system once it has left these shores as I have beforehand, and that is why we will be looking very carefully and rigorously at the current applications for export licences to Israel in the light of what has been used in the Occupied Territories'.[12]

5.41   On 24 October 2000 Amnesty International called on the UK government to suspend all exports or transfers of components, spares, servicing and equipment for US-supplied combat helicopters in Israel. More recently the organisation has called on the government to cease all transfers of lethal military equipment to the Israeli defence forces. This includes components for combat helicopters and tanks, small arms and light weapons, and ammunition, including air-to-surface rockets. This suspension should remain in force until the Israeli authorities demonstrate that the equipment will not be used to commit human rights violations in Israel, the Occupied Territories and the areas under the control of the Palestinian Authority.

5.42   Amnesty International welcomes the strengthening of end-user checks and risk assessment at the licensing stage. However, the organisation is concerned that without adequate post-export checks, the government will not know if end-user undertakings are being broken. The government must introduce a requirement to verify the delivery of goods to the stated purchaser, and replace the current *ad hoc* system of post-export checks by overseas officials with systematic monitoring by qualified staff.

Brokering

5.43   Arranging the sale and supply of weapons to countries subject to a binding UN arms embargo is banned under the 1946 United Nations Act. The 1998 white paper proposed to prohibit the brokering of weapons to countries subject to non-binding UN, EU and national embargoes, and those imposed by the Organisation for Security and Cooperation in Europe (OSCE).

5.44   The Export Control and Non-proliferation Bill will allow the government to impose controls on the brokering of controlled goods to all destinations. The government has proposed a list of goods to be controlled which broadly reflects the categories of weapons covered in limited arms embargoes. The QSC has argued that the controls should apply to the all categories covered by the Military List for the sake of operational and administrative simplicity.[13] Amnesty International agrees. Those engaged in brokering should be left in no doubt as to whether licensing is required for their activities. This policy should be consistent with that governing direct exports and should therefore apply to the same equipment.

5.45   Labour's election manifesto pledged the government to 'control the activities of arms brokers and traffickers wherever they are located'.[14] The powers in the bill enable the government to impose controls on arms brokering by UK passport holders operating from other countries. However, secondary legislation is required to define specific controls and make them enforceable. If the controls do not apply extra-territorially, unscrupulous brokers could readily circumvent them by conducting their business from other countries. German controls suffer from this weakness, as Brinley Salzmann, Exports Director of the Defence Manufacturers' Association informed the QSC: '[The German system] catches the good guys and the bad guys have moved to Cyprus.'[15] By contrast, US legislation controls brokering activities by US citizens operating overseas, and US officials believe that this has a significant deterrent effect.

Shipping agents

5.46   In recent years, a number of UK companies have been implicated in the transport of arms into regions of conflict. For example, in March 1999, a company based in Gibraltar reportedly brokered the sale of millions of pounds worth of arms from the Ukraine to rebel forces in Sierra Leone. The weapons, including Sam-7 missiles, anti-tank rockets, Kalashnikovs and grenade launchers, were allegedly shipped to Sierra Leone via Burkina Faso by a UK-based air freight company.[16]

5.47   While there is no explicit mention of shipping or transportation agents in the bill, clause 5, which covers brokering, is widely drawn and includes activities that facilitate the 'acquisition or disposal' of controlled goods. The bill would therefore permit the imposition of controls on shipping agents, but the government has indicated that it will not do so comprehensively: a British company would still be able to transport arms from Ukraine to Burkina Faso without a licence. The government has stated that controls will apply to shipping agents in relation to embargoed destinations, equipment used for torture and certain types of missiles. With regard to the transportation of controlled goods to other destinations, 'someone who was only involved in transport arrangements would not need a licence,' according to Nigel Griffiths, parliamentary under-secretary of state for small business and export control.[17]

5.48   The QSC has noted that 'it would ... seem perverse that those arranging for arms to be purchased for use in some area of conflict should be under a licensing regime, but not those responsible for arranging or undertaking their actual transfer.'[18] Amnesty International shares this view. The controls introduced to cover arms brokering must apply to the agents who transport the equipment. Each arms delivery should require a licence, even when the arms delivery takes place entirely in a third country. No licences should be granted for any arms delivery where there is a clear risk that the transfer will contribute to violations of human rights and humanitarian law.

Licensed production

5.49   Licensed production deals are increasingly supplementing and replacing direct exports. The number of licensed production facilities world-wide has grown dramatically in the last few decades and continues to grow year by year. Amnesty International is particularly concerned at the massive increase in the licensed production of small arms and light weapons. For decades, states such as the UK have allowed their small arms manufacturers to export their production capabilities all over the world. The global spread of small arms production facilities coupled with poor export controls in many countries is contributing to the proliferation and misuse of such weapons.

5.50   For example, violation of human rights in Turkey has been a concern of Amnesty International for many years. The *Amnesty International Report 2001* documents torture and ill-treatment of prisoners, possible unlawful killings by officials, rape in custody and other human rights violations. In 1995, Amnesty International called on governments to halt the transfers to Turkey of a range of arms and security equipment – including submachine guns, attack helicopters, surveillance equipment

and armoured vehicles – that could be used in human rights violations. In January 1998, defence industry publications *Jane's Defence Weekly* and *Defence News* reported that Heckler and Koch UK Nottingham, a subsidiary of BAE Systems, had won an $18 million contract to transfer technology for the local production of 200,000 5.56mm infantry rifles for the Turkish army. The rifles are reportedly being manufactured by Turkey's state-run artillery, small arms and ammunition maker Maki na ve Kimya Endustrisi Kurumu (MKEK).

5.51   MKEK are also making Heckler and Koch MP5 submachine guns under licence and have reportedly sold 1,000 of these to the Indonesian police, half of them at the height of the 1999 East Timor crisis.[19] Yet the UK government has refused several export licences to Indonesia for this category of weapon in the past three years. MKEK has previously exported arms to Northern Cyprus and Jordan, both notorious transhipment centres.

5.52   In its consultation document preceding the bill, the government recognised that the practice of licensed production must be regulated. However, the proposals put forward were weak and put the burden of regulation on UK companies instead of on the government. There is no explicit mention of licensed production in the bill itself. The QSC has stated: 'What is required is a system which ensures that the Government knows when a licensed production facility is being set up, and which ensures that the goods produced are not exported to countries or end-users where the UK would not licence them.'[20] The committee believed that statutory powers might be required to control licensed production overseas and recommended that the bill should provide for such powers to be taken in the future under secondary legislation).[21] As the bill does not explicitly provide those powers, it appears that the government will be unable to impose controls on licensed production overseas.

5.53   Amnesty International believes that the licensed production deal itself must be subject to scrutiny and approval. All licensed production deals should be treated as if they were standard physical arms transfers that would require an export licence. The licence determination procedure and end-use monitoring systems must be as rigorous as for standard exports. Specifically, applications for licensed production deals should be refused:
• where an export licence application for a direct weapons transfer would be refused;
• where the recipient state cannot demonstrate sufficient accountability in terms of export and end-use control;

- to states with a record of violating UN and other international arms embargoes.

5.54   We also believe that licensed production agreements should explicitly prohibit the export of equipment without the approval of the UK government, and should terminate if this requirement is breached. Overseas licensed producers must not be allowed to export arms manufactured under a UK licence to destinations to which the UK would not permit direct arms exports. We are concerned that under current proposals the UK government will be unable to stop such exports.

5.55   In addition, licensed production agreements should control the level of production. The quantity of arms to be produced and the length of the contract should be determined at the licensing stage and stringently monitored throughout the duration of the contract. If any of these conditions is breached, the licensed production agreement should be revoked and all further provision of related machine tools, parts, training and technology should be suspended. All export licences granted for licensed production deals and subsequent exports from overseas production facilities should be recorded in the annual report.

EU code of conduct

5.56   Under its presidency of the European Union, the UK government took the lead in pressing for the introduction of EU-wide arms controls. The objective was to 'set high common standards for arms exports from all EU states.' In June 1998, EU members agreed a European Code of Conduct on Arms Exports based broadly on the UK national export licensing criteria. Amnesty International welcomed the introduction of the EU code as an important step towards a harmonised EU strategic exports control system.

5.57   The code contains detailed criteria including the respect for human rights in the country of destination and the risk of diversion or re-export of arms to undesirable end-users. All EU member states must take the criteria into account when granting or refusing an export licence application.

5.58   The code also establishes a consultation mechanism among EU members. When one country refuses an export licence on the grounds of the code's criteria it must inform all the other member states why the licence application was refused. If another state wishes to take up the same contract as an 'essentially identical transaction' it must first consult the country that denied the application. By discouraging EU governments from agreeing to military contracts refused by other member states, it reduces the temptation for those who are approached first from entering into deals in the belief that if they do not, someone else will.

5.59   A weakness of the consultation mechanism is that it requires consultation only between the state that refused an application and the state that is considering granting a similar licence. If the code is to ensure common standards in arms exports from the EU, there should be consultation between all member states.

5.60   The code also suffers from the weaknesses identified in the UK system: lack of transparency, lack of parliamentary scrutiny, absence of a common system of end-use controls and the failure to control arms brokers, licensed production and mercenaries.

5.61   The code provides for an annual review of its operation and implementation. It requires EU members to submit yearly reports on their arms exports and their implementation of the code. There have been two annual reviews of the code, in October 1999 and December 2000.

5.62   The code also requires EU members to prepare and adopt 'a common list of military equipment covered by the code, based on similar national and international lists'. This was also identified as a priority for co-ordinated action in the first annual report into the code's implementation, in October 1999, which described a common control list as 'the cornerstone' of the code.

5.63   On 13 June 2000, the EU states adopted a common list of military equipment to be controlled. Amnesty International welcomes this development. Agreement on a common list of goods to be controlled is vital if high standards are to be achieved across the EU. Member states will now refer to the common control list in denial notifications, and are politically bound to ensure that their national legislation enables them to control the goods on the list.

5.64   The October 1999 annual report identified the need to define what constitutes an 'essentially identical transaction', but despite continuing discussion by the EU working party on conventional arms exports (COARM) agreement has not yet been reached. This is a matter of concern because establishing a common definition of an 'essentially identical transaction' is vital if the denial notification system is to function effectively.

5.65   The December 2000 report makes further recommendations, including 'the finalisation of a common list of non-military security and police equipment'. The European Commission is currently drafting a trade regulation to introduce a common control list for non-military security and police equipment. Amnesty International believes that this is particularly important given the discrepancies between EU countries' controls on this type of equipment. We believe that between them the common control lists should cover the full range of arms and security equipment, servicing, training and provision of personnel for military, security and police forces.

5.66   Acknowledging that the data provided in national annual reports, especially in statistical form, is hard to compare from one country to another, and that this 'hamper[s] joint efforts to achieve transparency', the December 2000 report calls on EU members to work towards the harmonisation of their annual reports.

5.67   The EU code states that it 'should be regarded as the minimum for the management of, and restraint in, conventional arms transfers by all EU Member States'. Amnesty International recognises and strongly welcomes the efforts of the UK government to establish and strengthen the code. The organisation urges the government to continue these efforts to strengthen the EU code to include stricter criteria, multilateral consultations when governments consider granting licences that others have refused, controls on arms brokering and on licensed production agreements, and processes that ensure transparency and accountability.

Small arms

5.68   Thousands of people are killed world-wide every year by weapons categorised as 'small arms' or 'light weapons' – handguns, assault rifles, sub-machine and machine-guns, grenades, mortars, shoulder-fired missiles and landmines. Many more are injured. Most of the victims are unarmed civilians who find themselves in the path of rival armies or criminal gangs. Transnational networks of brokers, dealers, financiers and transporters are the key players in small arms markets, yet most states do not even register them, let alone regulate their activities.

5.69   In response to the problem, the UN convened an international conference on the illicit trade in small arms and light weapons in July 2001. The aim of the conference was to seek agreement on a programme of action containing recommendations to governments. Amnesty International welcomed the initiative, which provided an important opportunity to address the proliferation and misuse of small arms.

5.70   The UK government played an active, constructive role in the EU and the wider international community in the run-up to the conference. The EU is to be commended for identifying the importance of regulating brokering, as Belgian foreign minister Louis Michel noted in describing the EU's common position when he addressed the UN conference: 'Brokering is a major problem in the context of illicit trade in small arms. For this reason we consider a legally binding instrument to be necessary here as well. Nor should transport and financing be forgotten. On this latter point, possible links between trafficking in arms and other kinds of illicit trade should be examined.'[22]

5.71   However, the Programme of Action adopted by the conference was disappointing. Canada, Norway and the EU countries pressed for agreement that small arms should not be exported where there is a real risk that they will be used to violate human rights or fuel foreign aggression. A number of governments including the USA, China, many members of the Association of South East Asian Nations (ASEAN), the Arab Group and South Africa blocked moves to secure such commitments. Amnesty International calls upon the UK government to continue its advocacy for stronger international control on the transfer of small arms.

Mercenaries and private security companies

5.72   There is long-standing international concern about human rights abuses committed by mercenaries, whether employed by governments and armed opposition groups or by private companies to protect their commercial interests. Mercenaries commonly operate outside the general systems of accountability that should govern the use of force in accordance with international law.

5.73   The UK has a long history of supplying mercenaries, training and other military and security services. Concerns about the activities of British mercenaries and security consultants have been raised, for example, by the Channel 4 *Dispatches* programme 'The War Business' in May 1998. The programme reported that personnel of the company Executive Outcomes were involved in the civil war in Angola and had committed grave human rights abuses, including the use of phosphorus bombs and the deliberate aerial bombardment of civilians in the market of San Pedro.

5.74   The legislation relating to mercenaries was passed in 1870 and is now outdated. In June 1998, Baroness Symons told the House of Lords that the government was 'examining a number of options for national domestic regulation of so-called private military companies operating out of the United Kingdom'.[23] The government did not subsequently put forward any proposals.

5.75   In 1999 the House of Commons foreign affairs committee inquired into the involvement of the UK security consultants Sandline International in Sierra Leone, and recommended that the government should publish a green paper (consultation document) outlining legislative options for the control of private military companies operating from the UK, its dependencies and the British islands.[24] In response, Robin Cook announced in April 1999 that the government would produce a green paper on mercenary activity by the end of November 2000. It did not do so.

5.76   Enrique Ballesteros, the UN special rapporteur (independent expert) on mercenaries, has described the failure to publish a consultation paper as 'a deplorable backward step' following revelations implicating former British soldiers with leading roles in companies offering military services.[25] According to Ballesteros, 'it is going to send a negative signal to other European countries who have been waiting for the British to introduce regulations before making similar moves'.[26]

5.77   Amnesty International urges the government to prepare, as a matter of priority, legislation to regulate the activities of mercenaries and private security companies operating from the UK. A key objective of the regulatory system must be to prevent human rights abuses. Those who provide services must be accountable for abuses committed and facilitated by their personnel.

Landmines

5.78   Anti-personnel landmines and other unexploded ordnance kill perhaps 10,000 people every year. As many again are injured, and nearly all survivors require at least one limb to be amputated. Eighty-five per cent of injured children die before they reach hospital. UK landmines are found in Afghanistan, Angola, Egypt, Jordan, Libya, Mozambique, Somalia and Zimbabwe.

5.79   In July 1998 the government ratified the Ottawa Convention, which prohibits anti-personnel mines, and introduced the Landmines Act 1998. The act prohibits the use, manufacture, export and possession of anti-personnel landmines. The Ottawa Convention entered into force on 1 March 1999, and by the end of the year the UK had destroyed most of its anti-personnel landmines. Four thousand were retained for training purposes, which is permitted under the terms of the convention. In 1999/2000 the government spent approximately £15 million on landmine clearance, including £6 million in Kosovo.[27]

5.80   There have been lapses in the implementation of the Landmines Act. For example, a Romanian company offered landmines for sale at the government-sponsored Defence Systems Equipment International exhibition in September 1999. At the same exhibition undercover journalists met an attaché of the Pakistan embassy who was there representing a state owned company called the Pakistan Ordnance Factory. Their company brochure advertised anti-personnel landmines for sale and the embassy attaché offered to send them to Sudan.

5.81   Perhaps of greater concern is that the UK government itself appears to be breaking the spirit of the Ottawa Convention. The convention aims to ban the manufacture and use of landmines that maim and kill humans, but different states interpret its language in different ways. According to the UK government, 'all UK weapons systems have been checked for compliance with the provisions of the Ottawa Convention. There are no weapons or munitions in the UK inventory that fall under the Ottawa definition of an anti-personnel mine. The UK is fully committed to a complete global ban on anti-personnel mines and will never again use these weapons'.[28]

5.82   However, the UK retains stocks of mines that could have anti-personnel capabilities because they contain anti-handling devices or sensitive fuses. According to an article in *The Observer*,[29] the UK has bought an estimated 60,000 Shielder L35A1 anti-tank mines and also holds quantities of Barmine and AT-2 mines. Shielder mines are not expressly prohibited by the Ottawa Convention as they are primarily anti-tank mines, but they have a highly sensitive magnetic fuse which causes them to detonate when stepped on.[30] Similarly, the AT-2 contains a highly sensitive anti-handling device and is classified by Italy as an anti-personnel mine, although it is not expressly prohibited by the convention.

5.83   The UK government has been reluctant to extend the application of the convention. According to non-governmental organisation Landmine Action, 'during discussions at the Standing Committee of Experts on the General Status and Operation of the Ottawa Convention in January 2000, nine states parties restated that under the Treaty's definitions and provisions, anti-vehicle mines with anti-handling devices which can be activated by the unintentional act of a person are banned'. Only the UK delegation publicly opposed a proposal to set up an expert group to examine the issue.[31] Amnesty International urges the UK government to assess the sensitivity of anti-vehicle mines in the UK inventory, publishing the results and destroying any mines that can be activated unintentionally. Pending the outcome of the technical assessment, the government should declare a moratorium on the manufacture, use and export of anti-vehicle mines likely to function as anti-personnel mines.

Corporate policies and practice

5.84   UK companies that source products from or invest in countries where human rights violations are prevalent risk involvement or complicity in those violations. Amnesty International believes that companies have a responsibility to minimise the risk of contributing to human rights violations and to use their legitimate influence to promote and protect human rights wherever they operate. Paying attention to human rights also serves commercial self-interest both overseas and at home. Abroad, countries that violate human rights generally offer a less stable climate for investment. Domestically, a company's reputation may be damaged by association with human rights violations. Those companies that have appropriate policy frameworks in place will find themselves in a stronger position to protect their assets and investments in the longer term. Without a firm commitment to upholding international human rights standards, companies are exposing themselves to risk.

First term initiatives

5.85   The UK government has an important

role in encouraging companies to adopt appropriate standards, and in creating a regulatory framework to enforce compliance. During its first term in office the government took several initiatives to influence the behaviour of companies with regard to human rights. They include:
• the Occupational Pension Schemes Regulation of July 2000. This stipulated that occupational pension funds in the UK must disclose in their statement of investment principles 'the extent to which, if at all, social, environmental or ethical considerations are taken into account in the selection, retention and realisation of investments';
• the support of the Department for International Development for the Ethical Trading Initiative, a cross-sectoral alliance of companies, NGOs and trade unions, has enabled some supermarkets, wholesalers and retailers to develop policies to improve working conditions in their supply chains by incorporating internationally agreed standards into their labour codes of practice;
• creating a new ministerial portfolio on corporate social responsiblity.

5.86   While these initiatives are helping to change business culture, they do not provide sufficient incentive for companies to change their practices. There is a substantial divergence between the expectations of society and the behaviour of companies with regard to human rights. This gap increases public mistrust of companies and gives impetus to the burgeoning anti-corporate movement.

5.87   Companies must be accountable for their impact on all those affected by their activities, and not only for serving their shareholders' interests. This will require fundamental changes in corporate governance and the establishment of a regulatory framework that enforces compliance.

5.88   A major review of company law that is currently being conducted has offered an opportunity to make significant changes in corporate accountability and governance. The opportunity was lost when the Company Law Review Steering Group rejected a 'pluralist stakeholder' approach which would have imposed on company directors a duty of care towards all those affected by a company's global operations.

5.89   The review also rejected a proposal that companies should be required to provide information about the social and environmental impact of their operations in their annual reports. Amnesty International believes that if companies were required to provide such details of their activities, and those of their subsidiaries and partnerships, they would be more accountable for their conduct and give affected communities, investors and other stakeholders greater opportunity to influence corporate policy.

Screening of export credit guarantees

5.90   Government policy, business and human rights intersect in the provision of export credit guarantees. The Export Credits Guarantee Department (ECGD) issued a new statement of business principles, which aims to take human rights impacts into account in the assessment of projects. This is reinforced by the ECGD's decision to publish an assessment of its performance in relation to the new business principles in its annual report. While Amnesty International welcomes these initiatives, the screening standards used to assess impact may not be adequate to give effect to the principles. In particular, it is not clear in what circumstances projects that might contribute to violations of international human rights standards would be deemed acceptable. Nor is it clear what the outcome would be if 'constructive engagement' on the part of the ECGD failed significantly to improve the social and environmental impact of projects.

Conflict diamonds and other resources

5.91   Amnesty International acknowledges the leading role of the Foreign and Commonwealth Office in pressing for tighter international controls over the trading of diamonds sourced from conflict zones in Africa. The links between the diamond trade and the flow of arms to these zones is a long-standing issue with implications far beyond the conflict in Sierra Leone. Other resources have also become the focus of conflict, for example coltan in the Democratic Republic of Congo. Amnesty International urges the government to contribute further to international efforts to prevent widespread human rights violations linked to resource exploitation.

Recommendations
Controlling the arms trade

▉ *EU ban on export of equipment for torture:* The government should continue to press for the EU to adopt as soon as possible a European-wide ban on the export of equipment used for torture.

▉ *Prior parliamentary scrutiny:* The government should introduce in the next parliamentary session a system of prior parliamentary scrutiny of applications for the export of arms and security equipment.

▉ *Information about exported arms and security equipment:* The government should provide additional information about strategic export licences granted or refused in the *Annual Report on Strategic Export Controls*. The information should include:
• complete and disaggregated alphanumeric codes, including sub-categories, as well as descriptive details indicating the type of arms and equipment licensed or refused for export;
• the quantity of arms and equipment;
• the end-user.

▉ *Verification of users and uses:* The government should require exporters to verify the delivery of goods to the stated purchasers. It should also introduce systematic monitoring of post-export users and uses by its own qualified staff.

▉ *Licensing of shipping agents:* The government should use powers provided under the Export Control and Non-proliferation Bill to impose controls on agents who transport arms and security equipment, even when the UK is not the country of origin, transit or destination. Every shipment should require a licence and a licence for the delivery of arms and security equipment should not be granted where there is a clear risk that the transfer will contribute to violations of human rights and humanitarian law.

Control of licensed production deals:
▉ Licensed production deals should be subject to the same forms of scrutiny and approval that apply to direct exports.

▉ Licensed production deals should not be permitted where the recipient state cannot demonstrate sufficient accountability in controlling export and end-use. Overseas licensed producers must not be allowed to export arms manufactured under a UK licence to destinations to which the UK would not permit direct arms exports.

▉ Licensed production agreements should specify the quantity of arms to be produced and the duration of the contract. If any terms of an agreement are breached, the agreement should be revoked and all further provision of related machine tools, parts, training and technology should be suspended.

▉ Permission granted for licensed production deals should be recorded in the annual report, as should details of any transfers of equipment from the overseas production facility.

▉ *EU code on control of arms exports:* The government should continue its efforts to

strengthen the EU code on arms exports to include:
• multilateral consultations when a government is considering granting a licence that others have refused;
• controls on arms brokering;
• controls on licensed production agreements; processes that ensure transparency and accountability.

■ *Control of trade in small arms*: The government should continue its advocacy for stronger international control on the transfer of small arms.

■ *Mercenaries:* The government should prepare, as a matter of priority, legislation to regulate the activities of mercenaries and private security companies operating from the UK.

■ *Landmines:* The government should assess the sensitivity of anti-vehicle mines in the UK inventory and destroy mines that can be activated unintentionally. Pending the outcome of the technical assessment, the government should declare a moratorium on the manufacture, use and export of anti-vehicle mines likely to function as anti-personnel mines.

Corporate policies and practice

UK company law
■ The government should revise UK company law to provide that:
• company directors have a duty to consider the interests of all those affected by their companies' operations, globally, not just the interests of shareholders;
directors have a responsibility for the activities of the companies' overseas subsidiaries and partnerships;
• companies are required to report on social, environmental and ethical aspects of their activities in their annual reports.

Screening export credit guarantees
■ The government should define in detail and publicly communicate:
• the screening procedures used by the ECGD to determine under what circumstances a project or transaction might reasonably be assumed to contribute to human rights violations;
• what actions will be taken when constructive engagement with a company on the part of ECGD fails to produce significant improvements in the social and environmental impact of a project.

Resource exploitation
■ The government should contribute to the development of international policies to prevent human rights violations linked to resource exploitation.

Appendix

Human rights in the United Kingdom

Briefing to the United Nations Human Rights Committee on Amnesty International's human rights concerns in the United Kingdom. July 2001

In the context of the UN Human Rights Committee's examination of the fifth periodic report of the United Kingdom (UK), in October 2001, under the International Covenant on Civil and Political Rights (ICCPR), Amnesty International draws committee members' attention to a summary of some issues which have been of concern to the organisation in recent years.

Human rights protection

There have been some major developments since the Human Rights Committee examined, in 1995, the UK's implementation of its obligations under the ICCPR.

The Human Rights Act, which came into effect in October 2000, incorporated most of the rights contained in the European Convention for the Protection of Human Rights and Fundamental Freedoms (the European Convention on Human Rights).
• Amnesty International believes that the government should ratify and incorporate Protocols 4, 7 and 12 of the European Convention on Human Rights; as well as ratify Article 13 of the European Convention which provides for an effective remedy for breaches of the Convention rights.
• Amnesty International believes that the Human Rights Act should be seen as a first step in the UK's incorporating a wide range of international human rights treaties and standards into domestic legislation. This should include the incorporation of the International Covenant on Civil and Political Rights and the ratification of the first Optional Protocol to the ICCPR.
The peace process in Northern Ireland has resulted in a number of positive developments: the repeated commitment within the Multi-Party Agreement of April 1998 to respect for human rights and the mechanisms outlined by the agreement to promote and protect human rights. A central mechanism was the creation of the Northern Ireland Human Rights Commission, which was set up in March 1999; one of its

Contents

Human rights protection

The right to life
Northern Ireland: Disputed killings by the security forces and collusion. England and Wales: Deaths in custody/disputed killings; Proposals for an independent investigatory body into police misconduct; Police handling of racist killings; Disputed deaths and cruel inhuman or degrading treatment or punishment; Ill-treatment by police officers.

The Terrorism Act

The right to fair trial
Equality of arms; The 'Diplock Courts'; Fair trial concerns.

The right to freedom of expression

Failure to protect vulnerable groups
Child soldiers. Asylum seekers: determination process; detention.

primary tasks has been to consult and draft proposals for a Bill of Rights for Northern Ireland. Another mechanism was the creation of the Equality Commission, which was set up later in the same year.

The agreement also proposed the initiation of independent reviewing bodies of policing and the criminal justice system in Northern Ireland. In March 2000, the *Review of the Criminal Justice System in Northern Ireland* was published. The 447-page review (with, additionally, 18 research reports) contained 294 recommendations, including the creation of a new prosecution service, the creation of an Independent Judicial Appointments Commission, the removal of overtly British symbols from court houses, the appointment of a minister for justice and a local attorney general. Legislation based on this review is likely to be introduced in the autumn of 2001.

In addition, in November 2000, the new Northern Ireland police ombudsperson, Nuala O'Loan, and her team of independent, civilian investigators began to function: to investigate independently, or to supervise police investigations of, allegations of police misconduct.

The review of policing, led by Chris Patten (known as the Patten Commission), resulted in the *Police (Northern Ireland) Act 2000*, which was passed into law in November 2000. Under this Act, the Royal Ulster Constabulary (RUC) will be renamed as the 'Police Service of Northern Ireland (incorporating the RUC)' and measures have been put in place to increase the recruitment of Catholics and women to the police service.
• Amnesty International is concerned that the Act failed to include all of the measures for increased police accountability which were recommended in the report produced by the Patten Commission. These included :
(a) increasing the powers of the civilian oversight body (a policing board) and of the police ombudsperson to initiate inquiries into police policies and practices;
(b) reflecting the Patten Commission's recommendation that human rights protection be at the heart of policing and that policing be carried out within the framework of international human rights norms and standards. For example, the oath to uphold human rights, which Patten had recommended should be taken by all new and serving officers, will only be taken by new officers.

The right to life *(Article 6)*
Northern Ireland: Disputed killings by the security forces and collusion

Since the mid-1980s Amnesty International has expressed concern about the government's failure to ensure that disputed killings, including by the security forces or with their alleged collusion, were investigated promptly, impartially, independently and thoroughly. Such failure resulted in violations of international human rights. The police investigations have been flawed in many cases; the prosecution authorities have failed to bring prosecutions in most cases; and inquests in Northern Ireland have failed to provide a forum for public scrutiny of the full circumstances of disputed killings and to examine the legality of law enforcement officials' actions.

Significantly in this context, the judgments delivered by the European Court of Human Rights in May 2001 highlight these concerns. The

unanimous rulings were made in four cases brought by the families of 11 people killed by security forces and one person killed by an armed Loyalist group with the alleged collusion of the security forces.[1] The European Court concluded that the UK had violated the right to life in Northern Ireland.[2]

Consistent with the concerns expressed by Amnesty International, the European Court found in all four cases that the procedures for investigating the use of lethal force by police officers failed to meet the requirements of Article 2 of the European Convention on Human Rights, which enshrines the right to life. It criticised the lack of independence of the investigating police officers from the officers implicated; the lack of public scrutiny; and the lack of information provided to the victims' families by the prosecution authorities about decisions not to bring prosecutions. Also, the Court criticised the fact that the inquest procedure in Northern Ireland does not allow any verdict or finding which could play an effective role in securing a prosecution of any criminal offence; and that people suspected of causing the death cannot be compelled to give evidence at an inquest. The court considered that the non- disclosure of witness statements to the victim's family prior to the witness appearing at the inquest prejudiced the families' participation in the inquest. It also was critical of delays in each case.

The landmark judgments effectively require the UK government to change the procedures by which it investigates killings in disputed circumstances, including criminal investigations, prosecution decision-making and the inquest system. They will have major repercussions not only for the families of the 12 victims of killings in disputed circumstances which the European Court examined, but also for many other cases in Northern Ireland, as well as procedures in the rest of the UK.

There are over a dozen inquests into disputed killings pending in Northern Ireland. The families of some people, who were killed by the security forces or by paramilitary groups in alleged collusion with members of the security forces, have waited many years for an inquest. However, such inquests cannot now proceed in light of the recent rulings.

Although Amnesty International welcomes the UK government's announcement in early 2001 of a two-year review of the inquest procedure, this will not alleviate the pressing need for families of the victims to have the full circumstances of the killings examined and publicly scrutinised in the near future. The government needs to urgently address these issues.

Patrick Finucane, a Catholic human rights lawyer, was shot dead in February 1989 by Loyalist paramilitaries. Since the early 1990s Amnesty International and other NGOs have called for a judicial inquiry into his killing, after allegations emerged of official collusion in his murder.[3] It has been alleged that MI5 (security services), RUC Special Branch and a secret military intelligence unit, all played a role. Questions are also posed about the extent of knowledge held by the Northern Ireland Office or Cabinet members concerning the operations of the various intelligence units.

Sir John Stevens was recalled to Northern Ireland for the third time in April 1999 to carry out an investigation into the murder of Patrick Finucane and other related matters of collusion (known as the 'Stevens 3' investigation).[4] Evidence has emerged that a secret military intelligence unit, known as the Force Research Unit (FRU), used an informer in the Ulster Defence Association (UDA, a Loyalist paramilitary group) to target and kill a number of people. Evidence has also emerged that in the case of Patrick Finucane, Loyalist informers passed information on the targeting of Patrick Finucane, before his killing, to both the RUC Special Branch and to the FRU. In October 2000 it was reported that Special Branch officers had blocked further investigation of a senior North Belfast UDA commander who admitted his part in the murder of Patrick Finucane to three RUC detectives in 1991.

To date only one person has been charged in connection with the murder of Patrick Finucane. William Stobie was initially charged in June 1999 with murder, although the charge was reduced on 30 August 2000 to aiding and abetting, counselling and procuring others to murder Patrick Finucane. Information on Stobie's role had been available to the police and to the Director of Public Prosecutions (DPP) in 1990, at which time a prosecution was not brought. William Stobie, a former UDA quartermaster, had admitted in police interviews that he supplied one of the weapons used; but he also insisted that at the time he was an agent of the RUC Special Branch and that he had kept Special Branch informed before and after the murder of the information he had received.
• Amnesty International is concerned that the current Stevens investigation is not examining all the killings that may have been carried out as a result of official collusion or acquiescence and urges the government to initiate a full, independent and public inquiry into the killing of Patrick Finucane and into all aspects of collusion.

Amnesty International is also concerned that the government is attempting to intimidate former members of intelligence units, journalists and newspapers from investigating and making public claims of illegal activities by state agents. The case of a former member of FRU, known as Martin Ingram, is an example. Ingram made startling revelations concerning the operations of FRU in the *Sunday Times* in November 1999. This resulted in a year-long police investigation of Martin Ingram and the *Sunday Times* journalist Liam Clarke, for breaching the Official Secrets Act. The Ministry of Defence also obtained an injunction against the *Sunday Times* to prevent the newspaper from publishing further disclosures by Martin Ingram. (See below for more information on the right to freedom of expression.)

Rosemary Nelson, a human rights lawyer, was killed by a Loyalist car bomb in Lurgan in March 1999.[5] In the face of calls for a fully independent investigation into her killing, in particular in view of the threats she had received prior to her death, the RUC chief constable appointed senior British officers to lead the police investigation. Colin Port, the deputy chief constable of the Norfolk police, has led the investigation since April 1999. Amnesty International was concerned that this investigation contained officers from the RUC, particularly in view of the fact that Rosemary Nelson had been threatened and intimidated by RUC officers, and urged that the investigation be totally independent. To date, although arrests have been made, no one has been charged in connection with the murder.

Amnesty International has been concerned by the lack of a prompt, thorough and impartial investigation into all the complaints of threats and intimidation made by Rosemary Nelson before her death; Rosemary Nelson had been allegedly threatened, through her clients, by RUC officers. The results of the internal police investigations have still not been made public. On 23 December 1999 the DPP decided not to prosecute anyone as a result of complaints Rosemary Nelson had made about threats issued against her by RUC officers. In May 2000 the Independent Commission on Police Complaints decided not to recommend disciplinary action against the RUC officers who allegedly threatened and intimidated Rosemary Nelson. Amnesty International believes that these decisions have not been made on the basis of a full and impartial investigation and urges that such an investigation be carried out. The organisation also notes that other complaints are still pending.

Amnesty International is also concerned that the investigation into the failure of the police and the authorities to protect Rosemary Nelson's right to life, despite the known threats to her life, has not been prompt, thorough and impartial.
• Amnesty International continues to urge an

independent public inquiry into the killing of Rosemary Nelson, because it believes that only such an inquiry can address all of the concerns which have arisen.

Robert Hamill: On 27 April 1997, Robert Hamill, a Catholic, aged 25 and the father of three children, was walking through the centre of Portadown with three companions when they were attacked by a crowd of around 30 Loyalist men and women. The two men were beaten and kicked savagely, and Robert was knocked unconscious almost immediately. The crowd continued to kick him as he lay on the ground while shouting sectarian abuse such as 'Die you Fenian [republican] bastard'. According to Robert Hamill's companions, four police officers who were sitting in a RUC jeep about six metres away did not intervene to stop the attack or come to their assistance. Having suffered a severe head injury, Robert Hamill never regained consciousness and died on 8 May 1997.

Initial reports issued by the RUC following the attack misleadingly claimed that there had been a battle between Loyalist and Republican factions in which it would not have been safe for the police to intervene, and that the police had come under attack. No evidence was collected at the scene of the incident and no one was arrested that evening or during the immediate period following the violent attack. The attack was investigated by RUC officers from Portadown RUC station, the same station as the RUC officers who failed to intervene in the attack. Following the death of Robert Hamill, six people were arrested and charged with his murder. However, by November 1997 all but one of the six suspects had been released. The only person to be brought to trial was Paul Hobson, who was acquitted of Robert Hamill's murder in March 1999 for lack of evidence. Paul Hobson was sentenced to four years' imprisonment for committing an affray.

After the Hamill family lodged a complaint against the RUC for their failure to act at the time of Robert Hamill's killing, a police investigation into the conduct of the four police officers at the scene was carried out under the supervision of the Independent Commission for Police Complaints (ICPC). The ICPC subsequently forwarded the investigation report to the Director of Public Prosecutions (DPP). Following the trial of Paul Hobson in March 1999, on 29 September 1999 the DPP decided not to bring criminal charges against any of the officers. The coroner leading the inquest into the death of Robert Hamill decided in June 2000 that he was unable to hold an inquest because he was unable to guarantee the safety of a key witness. In November 2000 the newly created Police Ombudsperson took over the supervision of the investigation from the ICPC.

Amnesty International is concerned about the alleged failure of RUC officers to intervene and protect Robert Hamill and his companions when they were attacked by a large group of Loyalists; about the failure of the RUC officers to provide first aid to Robert Hamill; about the failure of the RUC to impartially and promptly investigate the attack, including the failure to preserve the scene of crime, to secure forensic evidence and to make arrests promptly.
• Amnesty International is therefore calling for a full, independent and impartial inquiry to be carried out into the circumstances surrounding the killing of Robert Hamill and the role played by the RUC at the time of the incident and in the investigation.

England and Wales: Deaths in custody/disputed killings

Amnesty International has identified a pattern of deaths in police custody in England and Wales, due to excessive use of force and restraint techniques leading to asphyxia. In many incidents, the victims have also been subjected to ill-treatment. A large proportion of the victims have been from black or other ethnic minority communities. Amnesty International is concerned that the authorities have failed to carry out independent investigations into the full circumstances of each death; to make the results of the investigations public; and to bring to justice those allegedly responsible. This is coupled with an inquest system which is flawed. These failures have eroded public confidence in the criminal justice system. Amnesty International believes that the system of investigation and prosecution of disputed deaths in police custody is seriously flawed and is unsuitable to bring about impartial, thorough and transparent investigations and just prosecutions and is intrinsically biassed in favour of police officers.

Such systemic failures can best be understood through some illustrative cases, which Amnesty International has been monitoring. No one has yet been held accountable for any of these disputed deaths. (The cases are listed in chronological order.)

Christopher Alder, a black ex-paratrooper, died on 1 April 1998 in Queens Gardens Police Station, Hull, England, following his arrest in connection with a fight outside a nightclub. Five police officers were suspended from duty during the investigation into his death. In July 2000, an inquest jury returned a verdict of 'unlawful killing'. At the inquest it emerged that

Christopher Alder, who had been handcuffed behind his back, was found motionless on arrival at the police station. CCTV video evidence showed that he was dragged into the police station custody suite and placed face down on the floor, where he was left unconscious for over 10 minutes, his trousers around his knees as a result of being dragged. Even though Christopher Alder had been incontinent and his rattling breathing were audible from the video, the video showed that police officers speculated for several minutes that he might be faking, before calling an ambulance. Apart from removing the handcuffs shortly after arrival at the police station (reportedly after three minutes), none of the five police officers present at the custody suite attended to Christopher Alder for another seven minutes, until it was noted that he was not breathing anymore and resuscitation attempts were made, in vain. It was later found that Christopher Alder had blood and vomit in his mouth and may have been gasping for breath. Medical experts stated at the inquest that the cause of death was probably blocked air passages, which could have been cleared by emergency help. Flaws in the investigation also emerged at the inquest: Christopher Alder's clothes had been destroyed and the police officers' clothes had not been forensically checked.

In April 2001 the CPS decided not to bring manslaughter charges against the five officers allegedly involved. The CPS is still considering whether to bring charges for 'misconduct in public office amounting to wilful neglect'.

Roger Sylvester, a black man aged 30, fell into a coma on 11 January 1999 after being detained under the Mental Health Act and restrained by eight Metropolitan Police officers. He never regained consciousness and died a week later. Roger Sylvester was in front of his house in Tottenham, North London, reportedly naked and distressed, when police arrived, brought him to the ground, handcuffed him and put him in a police van to be taken to hospital. Several police officers allegedly restrained Roger Sylvester both while in the police van and at the hospital, where he finally collapsed. On 20 October 2000 the CPS ruled that no officer would be prosecuted, due to insufficient evidence.

In April 2001 the family of Roger Sylvester was granted permission for a full judicial review of the CPS decision. In May 2001 the Sylvester family sought disclosure of the investigation findings, and particularly of medical evidence, including post-mortem examination reports and statements made by hospital staff and of some pages of police officers' notebooks. The High Court refused to order the CPS to hand over

such documents, ruling that the family should access this information via an inquest. Counsel for the Sylvester family noted that at the inquest the police officers allegedly involved will be able to see all the evidence against them tested, while being allowed to exercise their right to silence, as they reportedly did throughout the investigation. In its ruling, the High Court also requested the investigating authorities to allow for a 'generous' pre-inquest disclosure of evidence, which they are otherwise legally entitled to withhold until 28 days prior to the inquest.

Harry Stanley was shot dead by an armed response unit of the London Metropolitan Police on 22 September 1999 in East London, while he was walking home with a table leg in a bag. He had just stopped in a pub where another customer, mistaking his Scottish accent for Irish and the table leg for a sawn-off shotgun, alerted the police. The police officers involved claimed that they shouted twice 'Stop, armed police', and shot Harry Stanley when he responded by turning around. He was struck by two bullets, one of which hit his head. Even though Harry Stanley had various documents on him and the shooting occurred one hundred yards from his home, it took about 18 hours for police officers in charge to identify him and to trace his family. This resulted in the family not having its medical and/or legal representative at the first post-mortem examination.

On 4 December 2000 the CPS announced that no criminal charges would be brought against the police officers who shot dead Harry Stanley, because their response was commensurate with the degree of risk they honestly believed they were facing. The family is applying for judicial review of the CPS decision and is asking the Metropolitan Police Commissioner to publish, in the public interest, the investigation report into the shooting.

Proposals for an independent investigatory body into police misconduct in England and Wales

In May 2000 following strong criticism expressed by lawyers, non-governmental organisations (including Amnesty International), national authorities and the European Committee for the Prevention of Torture over the past few years, the Home Office initiated a consultation on the reform of the investigation system into serious police misconduct and on the creation of an independent body to carry out such investigations. In the context of this consultation, Amnesty International published a document entitled *UK - Deaths in custody: lack of police accountability* (AI Index: EUR 45/42/00).

After an initial consultation, the government

published in December 2000 a second document for further comments by interested parties entitled *Complaints Against the Police. Framework for a New System*, which proposed a new system for investigating serious police misconduct, involving independent civilian investigators. The new body, the Independent Police Complaints Commission (IPCC), would have its own investigation teams, run by civilians and made up of a mix of police and non-police members. The most serious cases of alleged police misconduct (including deaths in custody, serious injuries, shootings and racist conduct), whether or not a complaint has been made, would be referred to the IPCC. In such cases, the IPCC would have the discretion to investigate independently the allegations or to supervise the police investigation.

Amnesty International welcomed the government's decision to reform the current system for investigating allegations of police officers carrying out human rights violations, including unlawful killings, excessive use of force, and torture and cruel, inhuman or degrading treatment.

Amnesty International has participated in the consultation exercise from the start, focusing particularly on the investigation and prosecution of controversial death in police custody cases.
• Amnesty international considers that the proposed investigatory body must be seen to be independent of the police force in investigating allegations of serious police misconduct in order to gain public legitimacy and credibility.
• International urges that the proposed legislation include the following:
(a) there should be agreed criteria for the acceptance and recording of complaints, and they should be publicly available;
(b) allegations of ill-treatment, harassment and cruel, inhuman or degrading treatment should be explicitly included, regardless of the seriousness of the injury, in the list of cases to be referred directly to the proposed IPCC for investigation. In each such instance the proposed IPCC should be responsible for determining whether to submit a case to the Crown Prosecution Service;
(c) the proposed IPCC should have the power to initiate investigations into patterns of alleged police misconduct, whether or not complaints have been lodged;
(d) the complainant and his/her legal representative should have the right to be present at disciplinary hearings and not to be excluded from them by the presiding officer, as should members of the proposed IPCC;
(e) information obtained from investigations should be disclosed to the victim or family of the victim, subject only to the harm test;
(f) the proposed IPCC should comply with and

uphold international human rights standards.

Police handling of racist killings

Amnesty International has been concerned that the police have failed to carry out prompt, thorough, and impartial investigations into suspicious deaths of people from black or other ethnic minorities. The failure of the Metropolitan Police to carry out such an investigation was examined by a public judicial inquiry in the case of Stephen Lawrence, aged 17, who was killed in 1993 by a group of white youths. The inquiry found that the investigation had been flawed 'by a combination of professional incompetence, institutional racism and a failure of leadership by senior officers'.

Another case which aroused public concern was that of Michael Menson, who died after being set on fire in a racist attack in January 1997. The police had initially treated the case as suicide, even though Michael Menson had made statements about the circumstances to his friends and hospital staff before dying. He was conscious for six days after the attack; during that time the police failed to interview him about the circumstances. Following a reinvestigation, begun in 1998, by the Metropolitan Police's Racial and Violent Crimes unit,[6] three men were charged in March 1999 with his murder. Two were convicted of manslaughter and the third of murder.

Ricky Reel died in October 1997 after drowning in the Thames river. The police failed to carry out a thorough and impartial investigation; and the Police Complaints Authority found three officers guilty of neglect of duty. An inquest jury in November 1999 returned an open verdict on the cause of death; the family believe he died as a result of a racist attack.

Disputed prison deaths and cruel, inhuman or degrading treatment or punishment *(Articles 2, 6, 7, 10, 14 and 22)*

Amnesty International is concerned that detainees in England and Wales, both on remand and convicted, have died while in prison custody or been subjected to torture or cruel, inhuman or degrading treatment or punishment; racist abuse; and medical neglect. The authorities have failed to protect detainees' fundamental human rights including the rights to life, to dignity, to physical and mental integrity, and to fair trial.

Although there have been very few deaths in recent years involving control and restraint methods by prison officers, the authorities have still failed to protect prisoners' rights to life and to physical and mental integrity. The number of suicides continues to be high: in 1999 there were 91 suicides and in 2000 there were 81; case after case demonstrates the authorities' failure to take adequate preventive measures, whether through ensuring adequate training of all prison staff in suicide-prevention methods, or through failing to provide adequate conditions and medical treatment as a preventive method.[7] Complaints by prisoners about the lack of adequate medical treatment are widespread. The conditions in which prisoners are held may amount to cruel, inhuman or degrading treatment. The Chief Inspector of Prisons has signalled that the long-term confinement of dangerous prisoners in solitary punishment cells is jeopardising their mental health and making them more disruptive. The continued practice of long periods of isolation or 'lock-up' (including up to 23 hours per day) and inadequate exercise and meaningful activity has also greatly affected the physical and mental well-being of prisoners. These violations of the right to physical and mental integrity are coupled with widespread allegations of torture and ill-treatment both by prison officers and by prisoners. Moreover, bullying and intimidation are also widespread, not only by prison officers of prisoners but also by prison officers of other members of staff. Even the Prison Service Director General referred last year to 'a culture of violence' in some prisons, which allowed officers to abuse prisoners with impunity. Many black and other ethnic minority prisoners allege that such treatment is often racially motivated. Internal prison inquiries have concluded that there was 'institutional racism' in some prisons, and the Commission of Racial Equality is currently investigating racism in three prisons. Of particular concern is the fact that juveniles under the age of 18 are subjected to all of the above-mentioned violations.

The system for dealing with prisoners' complaints of serious allegations of ill-treatment and other forms of abuse and for ensuring the accountability of prison staff, both management and officers, needs radical change for it to become effective. Inquests, which are the only form of public scrutiny and examination of any deaths in prison, are inadequate in addressing the full circumstances of such deaths and in scrutinising the legality of actions taken by public agents.[8]

What is most disturbing is the fact that all of the above violations have been documented thoroughly and regularly by the chief inspector of prisons, various NGOs and the prisons ombudsperson. Amnesty International is concerned by the government's failure, on the one hand to develop adequate guidelines and policies to ensure that prisoners' human rights are fully protected, and on the other hand to provide adequate resources to deal with systemic problems in order that the right to dignity, both of prisoners and prison staff, be protected.

Zahid Mubarek: In November 2000 the conviction of Robert Stewart, aged 20, for the murder of his cell mate, Zahid Mubarek, aged 19, on 21 March 2000 at Feltham Young Offender Institution and Remand Centre (YOI/RC), raised serious concerns about the wider context in which the murder took place. According to the evidence at the trial, Zahid Mubarek, of Pakistani origin, was put in the same cell as Robert Stewart even though prison officers were or should have been aware of Robert Stewart's racial prejudices and violent behaviour. Amnesty International also received allegations that the locking-up time for some wings at Feltham was 23 hours per day, with extremely limited facilities to carry out any meaningful or physical activity, and that many detainees lived in an atmosphere of intimidation, bullying and fear. In 1998 the chief inspector of prisons had conducted an inspection at Feltham, and had concluded that the conditions and treatment of the children and young prisoners, were, in many instances, totally unacceptable. Amnesty International considers that the detention of young people in the conditions described in his report constitute cruel, inhuman and degrading treatment.

• In December 2000 Amnesty International urged the government to establish a wide-ranging, independent and public inquiry into the circumstances of the killing of Zahid Mubarek, and into the failures of Feltham YOI/RC to protect the lives and well-being of prisoners in its care. Amnesty International also urged that the inquiry examine how the prison system deals with children and young offenders and the compatibility of its policies and treatment with international standards.

Alton Manning, a 33-year-old black remand prisoner, died in December 1995 after a struggle with officers in Blakenhurst Prison in Worcestershire, England.

In 1996 the Crown Prosecution Service (CPS) decided not to bring charges against any of the prison officers allegedly involved. In March 1998 an inquest jury ruled that Alton Manning had been unlawfully killed after prison officers restrained him in a neck-lock, leading to positional asphyxia, during a violent struggle. After the inquest, seven officers were suspended. The findings of the inquest were referred to the CPS for further consideration, but in 1999 the CPS confirmed that no prosecutions would be brought for Alton Manning's death. The matter was referred back to the CPS on 17 May 2000 by the Divisional Court, after the deceased's family brought a successful judicial review of the previous CPS decision not to bring charges. On 1 June 2001 the CPS again announced that it would not be prosecuting any prison officer for the death.

Ill-treatment by police officers

Amnesty International continues to receive allegations that people have been subjected to ill-treatment by police officers; many of the victims come from black or other ethnic minorities. The organisation is concerned that such allegations have not been investigated thoroughly, impartially and independently, and that the perpetrators of such ill-treatment have not been brought to justice, despite the frequent out-of-court settlements or court-awarded settlements for damages to the victims.

In February 1994 David Adams was subjected to ill-treatment both during arrest and at Castlereagh interrogation centre, Northern Ireland. He claimed he had been beaten and deliberately kicked so hard that his leg was broken; he suffered multiple injuries and was hospitalised. Several years later he was awarded £30,000 damages for assault by a judge. The DPP did not bring any prosecutions, despite critical comments by the judge. In 2001 David Adams lost a high court action against the DPP's decision not to prosecute RUC officers alleged to have ill-treated him.

The Terrorism Act

(Articles 2, 9, 14, 19, 26)

Amnesty International has expressed serious concerns about the *Terrorism Act* which was enacted in July 2000, and which makes permanent, temporary or emergency measures. Amnesty International considers that this legislation contains provisions which either directly contravene international human rights treaties to which UK is a party, or may result in violations of the rights not to be subjected to torture or ill-treatment, to fair trial and to freedom of expression and association. Some of these provisions were drawn from previous emergency or temporary legislation, which in the past facilitated serious abuse of human rights, as extensively documented by the organisation throughout the years.

The creation of a permanent distinct system of arrest, detention and prosecution relating to 'terrorist offences' may violate the internationally recognised right of all people to be equal before the courts. This different treatment is not based on the seriousness of the criminal act itself but rather on the alleged motivation behind the act, defined in the Act as 'political, religious or ideological'. Some of the provisions that Amnesty International is concerned about in particular are the following:

• the wide definition of 'terrorism' includes not only the use but also the threat of action involving serious violence against a person or serious damage to property or designed to seriously interfere or disrupt an electronic system. The purpose qualifying such an action or threat as terrorist, i.e. advancing a 'political, religious or ideological cause', is also very wide and open to subjective interpretation. The definition is vaguely worded and could be extended to include supporters of, for example, animal liberation or anti-nuclear campaigns and others. The lack of a clear definition gives cause for concern because the decision to bring a prosecution for such offences could be seen to be political;

• wide-ranging powers of arrest without warrant;

• denial of a detainee's access to a lawyer upon arrest: the right to legal assistance can be delayed, up to 48 hours, if the police believe the granting of this right may impede the investigation;

• the Act allows for a consultation between lawyer and detainee to be held 'in the sight and hearing' of a police officer, if a senior police officer has reasonable grounds to believe that such consultation would lead to interference with the investigation. Separate provisions, in relation to Scotland, similarly allow for an officer 'to be present during a consultation'. These powers breach international standards which require respect for the confidentiality of communications between lawyers and clients;

• the maximum period of detention without charge is seven days, with an extension of up to five days being granted by a judicial authority after the initial 48 hours. The provisions regarding judicial supervision of detention are still significantly weaker than under ordinary legislation. Under ordinary legislation, the maximum period of detention without charge is four days, with further 36-hour and 24-hour extensions being granted by a judicial authority after the initial 36 hours;

• provisions giving the Secretary of State the power to direct 'the place where a person is to be detained' are of concern if people arrested under this legislation could be detained at special interrogation centres, as opposed to designated police stations;

• the shifting of the burden of proof from the prosecution to the accused who must prove their innocence in various provisions of the Act; such provisions undermine the fundamental right to a presumption of innocence. For example, it is a criminal offence to collect or make a record of or possess information likely to be useful to a person committing or preparing an act of terrorism, including a photographic or electronic record; it is a defence for the accused to prove that he had a reasonable excuse for his action or possession;

• possible infringement of the right to freedom of expression and of association in some provisions of the Act, e.g. in the new offence of 'inciting terrorism overseas' which could be committed by words alone. There is a danger that prosecuting such 'inciters' may be prompted by overseas repressive governments targeting opponents based in this country. Thus these provisions may infringe the rights to freedom of expression and of association. Furthermore, there is concern that the right to fair trial may be infringed if people are charged on the basis of intelligence information provided by other governments or on the word of informants, if this information is then kept secret from the defendant through the use of public interest immunity certificates;

• Part VII of the Act, which extends for up to five years additional emergency powers applicable only in Northern Ireland, undermines the spirit of human rights protection in the Multi-Party Agreement of April 1998, in which the government committed itself 'to make progress towards the objective of as early a return as possible to normal security arrangements in Northern Ireland, consistent with the level of threat'. These provisions, which have resulted in unfair trials and other human rights violations, include the non-jury, single-judge 'Diplock Court' trials (see also below, the section on the Right to Fair Trial); a lower standard of admissibility for confessions as a basis for prosecution and conviction than in ordinary courts; the admissibility as evidence of the opinions of senior police officers that an accused person belongs or belonged to a proscribed organisation and the possibility for a court to draw inferences on the matter from the failure of the accused person to mention 'a fact which is material to the offence' and which he or she could 'reasonably be expected to mention'; and general police and armed forces powers of arrest, entry, search and seizures without a warrant.

• provisions allowing police officers to obtain court orders to force journalists to hand over to the police information in their possession which the police claim may be useful to their investigation. Amnesty International has been concerned in the past that the police have used similar emergency powers in order to intimidate journalists from pursuing certain lines of inquiry which may be embarrassing for the authorities; these cases have mainly involved investigative journalists who have refused to hand over information which was obtained in confidence from their sources or who have refused to reveal the name of their source. These journalists were exposing possible human rights violations by agents of the state and the attempts by the authorities to force journalists to reveal their sources or confidential information could have a chilling effect on freedom of expression.

Amnesty International is concerned that provisions in the Terrorism Act contravene UK obligations under international human rights law.

Furthermore, many provisions are open to abuse by law enforcement officials, and the Act fails to provide adequate safeguards against such abuse.

The right to fair trial *(Article 14)*
Equality of arms

Amnesty International sent an observer to the appeal hearing held in October 2000 in the case of Samar Alami and Jawad Botmeh. They had been sentenced in 1996 to 20 years' imprisonment after being convicted of conspiracy to cause explosions in 1994 at the Israeli Embassy and Balfour House in London. There was no direct evidence connecting them to the attacks and both had alibis. They stated that they were innocent of the charges. The appeal was based on the grounds that the convictions were unsafe in light of the evidence adduced at trial and material that appeared in the public domain since the trial, and of material available at trial which had not been shown to the defence or had been subjected to Public Interest Immunity certificates, thus blocking its disclosure. One of the grounds was based on revelations made by former MI5 agent, David Shayler, that the security services had received a warning before the bombing that an attack on the Israeli embassy was being planned and that this information had not been acted upon. The Court of Appeal judges decided to hold an ex-parte (closed to the defence) hearing to examine documents which had not been previously disclosed; after the hearing the judges ordered the disclosure of one piece of evidence. This consisted of a handwritten note outlining information received by the security services and Special Branch before the bombings that a terrorist organisation, unconnected to Samar Alami and Jawad Botmeh, was seeking information about the location and defences of the Israeli Embassy in London for a possible bombing attack. The note added that related intelligence after the bombings indicated that this particular organisation had not carried out the bombing. The note also explained that this information had not been disclosed to the trial judge by MI5 and Special Branch because of at least six counts of 'human error' and 'oversight'. After four days, the appeal hearing was adjourned until 2001 in order to allow the defence to make further inquiries into the sole piece of evidence disclosed at the appeal hearing as well as other evidence that had come to light during the time of the hearing.

Amnesty International was concerned that the two convicted people had been denied full disclosure, both during and after the trial, not only of the above information, but also of other crucial evidence which had been blocked by

Public Interest Immunity certificates. The organisation believes that failure to disclose crucial evidence violates the appellants' right to a fair trial. Amnesty International was also concerned that the appeal court proceeded with an *ex parte* hearing, ie in the absence of the defence team, which was not followed by full disclosure. The case of Samar Alami and Jawad Botmeh also highlights some of the dangers of issuing Public Interest Immunity certificates and raises questions about the accountability of the intelligence services.

The 'Diplock Courts' (Northern Ireland)

Amnesty International is concerned that the *Terrorism Act 2000* contains, under Part VII of the Act, additional emergency powers which are applicable only in Northern Ireland. Some provisions, which have resulted in unfair trials, include the non-jury, single-judge 'Diplock Court' trials, and a lower standard of admissibility for confessions as a basis for prosecution and conviction than in ordinary courts. The 'juryless' system, combined with the lower standard for the admission of evidence, is incompatible with the right to a fair trial.

• Amnesty International has documented, since the early 1980s, concerns about unfair procedures in the 'Diplock Courts' and has, more recently, called for them to be abolished. The organisation believes that the continuing existence of a special court is normalising what is intended under national law to be an exceptional and temporary measure and is contrary to international law.

Fair trial concerns: justice delayed

Amnesty International has been concerned about the long delays for victims of miscarriages of justice in obtaining justice. In Northern Ireland, one of the particular problems has been the difficulties people have faced in obtaining access to trial documents, in particular police interview notes, in order to carry out ESDA (electrostatic deposition analysis) tests on them to verify whether they were written contemporaneously. In October 1999, the Northern Ireland Appeal Court quashed the convictions of Billy Gorman and Paddy McKinney, who had been convicted for the murder of a police officer in 1974, after ESDA tests showed that police officers had rewritten and significantly altered interview notes. Gorman was 14 and McKinney 17 at the time of the killing. The case was re-opened because they had been convicted on the basis of these notes. Although the results of the ESDA tests were available in December 1994, the two appellants waited another five years before their convictions were quashed.

Fair trial concerns: the right to silence

Amnesty International has been concerned about the curtailment of the right of an accused to remain silent when questioned or charged and at trial. Under the Criminal Justice and Public Order Act 1994, a court or jury can draw inferences from an accused person's failure to mention facts when questioned before or on being charged. Inferences can also be drawn from an accused person's silence at trial, if he or she refuses to give evidence or to answer any question 'without good cause'.

Amnesty International believes that the right to remain silent during interrogation and at trial is a safeguard for the international standard of the presumption of innocence. Its curtailment can lead to the shifting of the burden of proof and to a form of coercion to give information or to testify.

'National security' detention/deportations

The European Court of Human Rights ruled in November 1996 that the government's attempt to deport Karamjit Singh Chahal to India was in violation of the European Convention for the Protection of Human Rights and Fundamental Freedoms. He had been detained since 1990 on a decision by the Secretary of State that he should be deported on 'national security' grounds since 1990. As a Sikh activist, believing that he would be a victim of torture or death if he was returned to India, Karamjit Singh Chahal applied for asylum. This application was refused.

Due to the claim of national security, he had no rights of appeal. Instead, he was only able to seek review by a panel, known as the 'three wise men', whose advice on the matter to the Secretary of State was not binding. In addition, he was not informed of the details of the allegations against him, was not entitled to representation by lawyers at the hearing and was not given a copy of the advice that the three wise men gave to the Home Secretary.

The European Court stated that the prohibition of torture was paramount and that allegations of national security risk were immaterial to a determination of whether a person faced risk of torture if refouled. The Court further ruled that the hearing before an advisory panel of three people did not satisfy the Convention's right to have one's detention scrutinised by a judicial authority, and that Karamjit Singh Chahal's detention had therefore been unlawful. Karamjit Singh Chahal was released immediately after the judgment. Subsequently, other people detained under the same provisions were released, including Sezai Ucar and Raghbir Singh.

In response to the judgment of the European Court in the Chahal case, new legislation, the Special Immigration Appeals Commission Act, was enacted in December 1997. This Act establishes a right of appeal where the Home Secretary has made a decision to deport or exclude a person, including on national security grounds. The appeal is heard by a Commission. Its decision is binding on the Secretary of State, though it may grant leave to appeal its decisions to a court. Under the Act, the Lord Chancellor has the authority to make rules for the conduct of the appeals, which are assented to by Parliament. Amnesty International has noted with concern that the statute and rules permit the proceedings to take place without the potential deportee or their counsel being provided with all of the reasons for the decision to deport or exclude. In addition these rules permit the Commission to hold all or part of the proceedings without either the potential deportee or their counsel being present. If such *in camera* proceedings are held, an advocate is appointed from a panel chosen by the Attorney General to represent the interests of the potential deportee. The advocate, however, may not communicate with the deportee or their counsel, after they have been provided with information about the case, without leave from the Commission. Before decisions are made on the basis of proceedings from which the deportee and their counsel have been excluded, a summary of the submissions and evidence and absent information about sensitive material must be provided.

The right to freedom of expression *(Article 19)*

Amnesty International is concerned that the government is attempting to prosecute former members of intelligence units and journalists under the Official Secrets Act; such threats of prosecutions may have a chilling effect on whistleblowers, journalists and newspapers from investigating and making public claims of human rights violations or illegal activities by state agents.

Amnesty International has been monitoring the case of David Shayler, a former MI5 (intelligence) officer who made a series of allegations in 1997 and thereafter about the activities of security and intelligence agencies. Some of the allegations concerned illegal activities by the security services. His allegations were printed in the newspaper the *Mail on Sunday* in August 1997. The government sought to extradite David Shayler from France to face a

criminal prosecution from the publishers of the *Mail on Sunday* for causing 'injury to the national interest'. In March 2000, a court ordered the *Guardian* and the *Observer* to comply with an MI5 order to hand over documents and e-mails relating to contacts with David Shayler, and to assist in the prosecution of David Shayler. The *Observer* had published information about an alleged MI6 plot to assassinate Libyan leader Mu'ammar al-Gaddafi. *Observer* journalist Martin Bright and its editor Roger Alton were investigated for contravening the Official Secrets Act by receiving and publishing the damaging disclosures. In May 2000 the newspapers were granted the right to challenge the court orders. David Shayler returned to the UK in August 2000 to face charges under the Official Secrets Act. The trial is pending.

Charges under the Official Secrets Act were also brought in 1998 against a former army general, Nigel Wylde, who provided information to journalist Tony Geraghty. Geraghty was charged for his book, *The Irish War*, which included information about the extent of computer-assisted surveillance of the population in Northern Ireland. The charges were dropped against journalist Tony Geraghty. Nigel Wylde was acquitted in November 2000 after the prosecution offered no evidence.

In May 2000, the UN Special Rapporteur for Freedom of Expression and Opinion, Abid Hussein, issued a lengthy report which was critical of provisions and practices which limit freedom of expression in the UK.

The *Freedom of Information Act* was passed in November 2000 and will come into force in 2002. Campaigners who called for stronger legislation noted that the Act provides for a 'public interest' test for disclosure of requested information. However, they were also critical of the provisions for exemptions from disclosure in some areas, including the formulation of government policy and all information gathered during an investigation which could have led to a prosecution. Decisions by public authorities are reviewed by the Information Commissioner. If the commissioner orders disclosure in the case of decisions made on the basis of prejudice-tested exemptions, such an order cannot be vetoed by ministers, but where the commissioner orders disclosure on public interest grounds from government departments, cabinet ministers can veto such an order. Campaigners were critical of the existence of the veto and of the class exemptions, both of which had been rejected in the government's original white paper. The devolved government in Scotland was preparing its own legislation on freedom of information which would pertain to those issues which are under its devolved responsibility.

The *Regulation of Investigatory Powers Act*, enacted in July 2000, legalised a variety of intrusive surveillance techniques, covert use of informants and agents, and the interception of communications.
• Amnesty International criticised the legislation for failing to provide sufficient safeguards, including judicial oversight (e.g., judicial scrutiny of warrants), to ensure accountability and protection of human rights. AI believes that some provisions could violate the rights to privacy and fair trial, and could have a chilling effect on the rights to freedom of expression and association.

Failure to protect vulnerable groups

Child soldiers *(Articles 6, 7)*

In November 2000 Amnesty International called on the UK to stop its policy of deploying under-18s into hostilities, as it launched a new report *United Kingdom: U-18s: Report on the Recruitment and Deployment of Child Soldiers* (AI Index: EUR 45/57/00). The UK has the lowest deployment age in Europe and it is the only European country to routinely send under-18s into armed conflict situations. The report gave examples of how recruitment and deployment of under-18-year-olds threatened their right to life and to their physical and mental integrity. Children can be recruited into the armed forces from the age of 16 and can be deployed into the battlefield from the age of 17. Two 17-year-old soldiers and one 18-year-old on the day of his birthday died in the Falklands war; two 17-year-olds died during the Gulf war. Other risks included injuries and deaths during strenuous training exercises, and being subjected to bullying and ill-treatment by other soldiers and by superiors. In recent years there has been a sharp increase in the annual recruitment of under-18s in the UK where there is no conscription, and children have been openly targeted by recruitment campaigns of the Ministry of Defence, for example, through the distribution of video-games. Between March 1998 and March 1999, 9,466 under-18s were recruited to the UK armed forces. In September 2000, the UK signed the Optional Protocol to the Convention on the Rights of the Child on the involvement of children in armed conflicts, and added a declaration which AI believes undermines the spirit of the Optional Protocol.
• Amnesty International believes the UK should ratify the Optional Protocol promptly without any reservation.

Asylum-seekers *(Articles 7, 10 and 14)*
Determination process

Amnesty International believes that every asylum claim should be looked at on its individual merits and is gravely concerned that 26,630 asylum applicants in 2000 were refused asylum on non-compliance grounds. This is 25,545 more than recorded during the previous year. Applicants are refused on non-compliance grounds for procedural reasons including failing to meet the tight deadlines on returning their Statement of Evidence Form rather than on the merits of their claim. There are many reasons as to why individual applicants may have difficulty in returning their Statement of Evidence Form in time, including being dispersed to a location where there is little access to quality legal advice and representation and the form having to be completed in English.

Detention of asylum-seekers in the UK

Hundreds of asylum-seekers are detained in the UK at any given time, many at the initial stages of their asylum claim, but current detention statistics do not distinguish between asylum-seekers and others detained under Immigration Act powers. Amnesty International believes that large numbers of asylum-seekers are detained for reasons which are contrary to those set out in international legal standards.

Oakington detention centre opened in March 2000 and by early May 2001, 7000 people had been processed at Oakington. Applicants from one of a list of countries may be referred to Oakington, where it appears that in addition to the existing detention criteria, their application can be decided quickly including those which may be certified as manifestly unfounded and there are not other circumstances which would make them unsuitable for the Oakington process. As of April 2001 the list of nationalities considered potentially suitable for Oakington are: Albania, Bangladesh, Bolivia, Brazil, Cameroon, China, Ivory Coast (temporarily suspended) Czech Republic, Estonia, Ghana, Hungary, India, Iraq, Kenya, Latvia, Lithuania, Nigeria, Pakistan, Poland, Romania, Slovakia, Slovenia, Tanzania, Ukraine, Uganda, Federal Republic of Yugoslavia, Zimbabwe. Operational constraints, for example, the availability of interpreters, limit the range of nationalities that can in practice be dealt with at Oakington at any one time. The decision-making process at Oakington is completed in seven days except for exceptional cases (legal advice and representation with interpretation facilities are on site). The majority of asylum applicants are refused. In February 2001, 20 percent of those who chose to appeal against refusal were transferred to other detention centres.

The government announced recently that by the autumn of 2001 there should be 2,790 detention centre places (including Oakington). However, many asylum-seekers are also detained in ordinary prisons; the government has set aside 500 additional places in prisons for immigration detention.

The two automatic bail hearings for those detained under Immigration Act powers due to come into force in April 2001 were initially deferred until October but have been deferred again.

Endnotes

International diplomacy

1 FCO *Mission Statement*, 12 May 1997, see http://www.fco.gov.uk/directory/dynpage.asp?Page=26

2 'Human Rights: A priority of Britain's foreign policy', speech by the foreign secretary in the foreign office, London, 28 March 2001.

3 *Official Report*, 22 June 2001, col 281.

4 DFID, *Realising human rights for poor people*, October 2000, para 3.5.

5 http://www.mod.uk/index.php3?page=180

6 Sixth Report from the International Development Committee, Session 1999-2000, ECGD, *Developmental Issues and the Ilisu Dam, HC 211, Minutes of Evidence*, Question 10. See also Questions 9, 11, 12,13 and 19.

7 Sixth Report from the International Development Committee, Session 1999-2000, paragraph 15.

8 Fourth Special Report from the International Development Committee, Session 1999-2000, *Exchange of Letters Concerning the Ilisu Dam, HC 813*. Letter to the chairman of the committee from Keith Vaz MP, minister for Europe.

9 *Ibid*, Letter to Keith Vaz MP, minister for Europe, from the chairman of the committee.

10 Seventh Special Report from the International Development Select Committee, Session 1999-2000, *ECGD, Developmental Issues and the Ilisu Dam, HC 293, Appendix: Government Response to the Committee's Report on ECGD*.

11 *Ibid*.

12 Fifth Report from the International Development Committee, Session 2000-2001, *ECGD, Developmental Issues and the Ilisu Dam: Further Report, HC 395*, para 8.

13 *Ibid*, para 9.

14 Fourth Special Report from the International Development Committee, Session 2000-2001, *ECGD, Developmental Issues and the Ilisu Dam: Further Report, HC 351. Appendix, Government Response to the Committee's Report*.

15 Fifth Report from the International Development Committee, Session 2000-2001, ECGD, *Developmental Issues and the Ilisu Dam: Further Report, HC 395, Appendix Annex B; Summary of Exchanges Between FCO and DTI/ECGD on Ilisu Dam*.

16 Fourth Special Report from the International Development Committee, Session 2000-2001, *ECGD, Developmental Issues and the Ilisu Dam: Further Report, HC 351. Appendix, Government Response to the Committee's Report*.

17 Speech by FCO minister of state, John Battle, at the UNHRC, Geneva, 22 March 2001.

18 Speech by Robin Cook, in the foreign office, London, 28 March 2001.

International justice

1 Preamble to the Rome Statute for an International Criminal Court.

2 Quoted in Antony Barnett and Andy McSmith, 'Pinochet: Straw may have misled MPs', *The Observer*, 16 January 2000.

3 *Official Report*, 12 January 2000, Col 278. Mr Straw subsequently set the record straight in a statement to the House of Commons. He said: 'It should be pointed out that the clinicians were not expected, in reaching their conclusions, to take responsibility for the legal test of fitness for trial, nor does the Secretary of State consider them to have done so. Their function was to ascertain the clinical facts. The test of fitness for trial which has been applied, both in framing their instructions and in assessing their report, is the responsibility of the Secretary of State, who in turn has drawn extensively upon the opinions of his legal advisers.' (*Official Report*, 2 March 2000).

4 MoD *Performance Report 1999/2000*.

5 *Official Report*, 24 November 1999, Col 148W.

6 The International Human Rights Committee of the Law Society for England and Wales, *Report of the Law Society Delegation to the International Criminal Tribunal for Rwanda, Arusha, Tanzania, 29 May- 2 June 2000*.

7 Quoted by Elizabeth Neuffer, 'Clinton Backs treaty for justice tribunal, Helms to fight war crimes pact', *The Boston Globe*, pA13 (date not known).

Asylum policy

1 Home Office Immigration and Nationality Directorate, *Report on the Asylum Decision Process Consultancy*, Vantagepoint. July 1999.

2 *"Cell Culture": The Detention and Imprisonment of Asylum-seekers in the UK*.

3 *Deciding to detain*, Institute of Criminology, University of Cambridge, 2000.

4 Report on the visit of the Working Group on Arbitrary Detention, 18 December 1998.

5 UNHCR EXCOM Conclusion 44 (f).

6 'Prison inspector attacks jailing of asylum seekers', *The Independent*, 22 January 2001.

Business and human rights

1 *Stopping the Torture Trade.* Amnesty International. ACT 40/002/2001
2 'Shame of British firms who trade in torture', *The Observer*, 10 September 2000.
3 *IPSE 2000 Showguide*, p6.
4 *Niton Equipment Professional Buying Guide*, p22.
5 Cm 5141. *Strategic Export Controls: Annual Report for 1999 and Parliamentary Prior Scrutiny. Response of the Secretaries of State.* July 2001.
6 DMA response to the Green Paper on Strategic Export Controls, as cited in Trade and Industry Select Committee Second Report HC 65, December 1998, *Minutes of Evidence.*
7 *Strategic Export Controls – Annual Report 2000.*
8 Defence, foreign affairs, international development and trade and industry committees, Third, Second and Seventh Report. *Strategic export controls: annual report for 1999 and parliamentary prior scrutiny*, March 2001.
9 QSC *Minutes of Evidence*, 25 April 2001, in QSC report HC 445 q226.
10 For example, see Amnesty International, *Israel and the Occupied Territories. State Assassination and other unlawful killings.* MDE 15/005/2001.
11 Peter Hain MP, 15 January 2001. *Hansard*, 18 January 2001, col.317W.
12 Robin Cook, *Minutes of Evidence*, 30 January 2001.
13 QSC report HC445, para 97.
14 *Ambitions for Britain*, Labour manifesto 2001.
15 QSC report HC 445, *Minutes of Evidence*, p20, q85, May 2001.
16 'Missiles for rebels "flown to Africa by British firm"', *The Independent*, 16 May 2000.
17 Letter to the UK Working Group on Arms, 27 July 2001.
18 QSC report HC445, para. 99, May 2001.
19 Channel 4 *Dispatches* programme, 'Licensed to Kill', 9 December 1999.
20 QSC report HC 445, para 106, May 2001.
21 QSC report HC445, para 106, May 2001.
22 UN Conference on the Illicit Trade in Small Arms and Light Weapons in all its Aspects, statement by HE Mr Louis Michel, deputy prime minister and minister of foreign affairs of Belgium, on behalf of the European Union, New York, 9 July 2001.
23 Lords *Hansard*, 30 June 1998, col WA65.
24 Foreign Affairs Committee Second Report, HC 116-I, 9 February 1999.
25 *Financial Times*, 18 April 2001.
26 *Financial Times*, 18 April 2001.
27 Landmine Action, http://www.landmineaction.org
28 (*Hansard*, 19 October 1999, col 420.
29 'Britain accused of stockpiling lethal landmines', *The Observer*, 19 November 2000.
30 Lords *Hansard*, 17 July 1998, col 505.
31 *Alternative Anti-personnel mines: the next generations*, Landmine Action, March 2001.

Appendix
Human rights in the United Kingdom

1 *Hugh Jordan v. the UK* (no. 24746/94); *McKerr v. the UK* (no. 28883/95); *Kelly and others v. the UK* (no. 30054/96); and *Shanaghan v. the UK* (no. 37715/97).
2 The government is still deciding whether to appeal the European Court's judgments.
3 See Amnesty International documents *Political Killings in Northern Ireland*, AI Index: EUR 45/01/94, and *Patrick Finucane's Killing: Official collusion and cover-up*, AI Index: EUR 45/26/00. See also the *Report on the mission of the Special Rapporteur to the UK*, 5 March 1998, E/CN.4/1998/39/Add.4 and subsequent annual reports, in which Special Rapporteur Param Cumaraswamy concluded 'that the RUC has engaged in activities which constitute intimidation [of lawyers], hindrance, harassment or improper interference'. He urged the authorities to conduct an independent and impartial investigation of all threats to legal counsel; he also recommended that the government initiate an independent judicial inquiry into the circumstances of the killing of Patrick Finucane.
4 See *United Kingdom: Political Killings in Northern Ireland*, AI Index: EUR 45/01/94, for details about the previous two investigations by Sir John Stevens. Sir John Stevens is currently the Commissioner of the Metropolitan Police, London. In December 1999 Deputy Assistant Commissioner Hugh Orde took over the day-to-day control of the 'Stevens 3' investigation (Sir John Stevens became the Commissioner for the Metropolitan Police shortly afterwards).
5 See Amnesty International's report: *Northern Ireland: The Killing of Human Rights Defender Rosemary Nelson*, AI Index: EUR 45/22/99.
6 The unit was set up in the wake of the Stephen Lawrence inquiry.
7 See *Keenan v. UK*, in which the European Court of Human Rights ruled in April 2001 that the failure to provide adequate medical care, psychiatric input and monitoring amounted to cruel, inhuman or degrading treatment and a violation of Article 3 of the European Convention on Human Rights.
8 *Keenan v. UK* - the European Court of Human Rights judgment of 3 April 2001 ruled that the inquest did not provide a remedy for determining the liability of the authorities for any alleged mistreatment, or for providing compensation.

The work of Amnesty International

Vision and mission

Amnesty International's vision is of a world in which every person enjoys all of the human rights enshrined in the Universal Declaration of Human Rights and other international human rights standards.

In pursuit of this vision, Amnesty International's mission is to undertake research and action focused on preventing and ending grave abuses of the rights to physical and mental integrity, freedom of conscience and expression, and freedom from discrimination, within the context of its work to promote all human rights.

Core values

Amnesty International forms a global community of human rights defenders with the principles of international solidarity, effective action for the individual victim, global coverage, the universality and indivisibility of human rights, impartiality and independence, and democracy and mutual respect.

Methods

Amnesty International addresses governments, intergovernmental organisations, armed political groups, companies, and other non-state actors. Amnesty International seeks to disclose human rights abuses accurately, quickly and persistently. It systematically and impartially researches the facts of individual cases and patterns of human rights abuses. These findings are publicised, and members, supporters and staff mobilise public pressure on governments and others to stop the abuses.

In addition to its work on specific abuses of human rights, Amnesty International urges all governments to observe the rule of law, and to ratify and implement human rights standards; it carries out a wide range of human rights educational activities; and it encourages intergovernmental organisations, individuals, and all organs of society to support and respect human rights.

Organisation

Amnesty International has over a million members in over 160 countries and territories. There are more than 4,300 local Amnesty International groups registered with the International Secretariat and several thousand professional and other groups, including over 3,400 youth and student groups, in more than 105 countries and territories in Africa, the Americas, Asia, Europe and the Middle East. Amnesty International has formal relations with the United Nations Economic and Social Council; the United Nations Educational, Scientific and Cultural Organisation; the Council of Europe; the Organisation of American States; the Organisation of African Unity; and the Inter-Parliamentary Union.